Serpentine Gallery

TROLLEY BOOKS 2005

SERPENTINE GALLERY
PAVILION 2005 DESIGNED BY **ÁLVARO SIZA**
**EDUARDO SOUTO DE MOURA**
WITH **CECIL BALMOND** - ARUP

Supported by        Supply and Fabrication        Integrated Design        Advisors

Member of Finnforest Corporation

# PAVILION

PAVILION: Portable accommodation; tent; hut; isolated construction, in the centre or on the sides of the main body of a building; small house; the wider edge of some wind instruments; pergola; flag; standard; naval symbol of nationality; naval strength of a country; bed canopy; sacrarium curtain; cartilaginous outer part of the auditory channel. *Encyclopaedia Verbo*

From this I extract the definition 'isolated construction, in the centre or on the sides of the main body of the building'.
The Pavilion leans towards the Neo-classical building like an animal with its paws riveted to the ground, tense with the desire to approach, but nevertheless restrained. Its back is distended, its hair standing on end. It glances sideways, with antennae twitching towards the building. It obliges it to define a space. It has to stop, lowering its head; it cannot go forward. But will it eat the building one day?

It allows passers-by to cross over it, discloses its brick floor for their enjoyment. It offers up chairs, tables, shade.
Lazy, but restless, it scatters a golden light that puts its stamp on the London sky – peaceful in its corner of the world.
No building can remain isolated, even if it wants to. In this world there are no deserts or far-off things.

Álvaro Siza
Porto, 2 March 2005

Serpentine Gallery
Pavilion 2005
Designed by Álvaro Siza
and Eduardo Souto de
Moura with Cecil
Balmond – Arup

# CONTENTS

# SUPPORTERS' FOREWORDS

Eurex is delighted to be collaborating with the Serpentine Gallery on the Pavilion designed by Álvaro Siza and Eduardo Souto de Moura with Cecil Balmond of Arup.

Eurex is the world's leading derivatives exchange. Its commitment is to innovation and pushing the boundaries of financial services worldwide. We stand for open, democratic access to financial markets and for connecting people across borders. In this spirit of community, Eurex has forged an association with one of London's finest and most accessible contemporary art galleries.

By supporting the Serpentine Gallery Pavilion 2005, Eurex is proud to play a central role in realizing one of London's most dynamic cultural events.

Rudolf Ferscha
Chief Executive Office
Eurex

Finnforest Merk is honoured to be collaborating with the Serpentine Gallery on this year's Pavilion, designed by the renowned Portuguese architects Álvaro Siza and Eduardo Souto de Moura with Cecil Balmond of Arup. The Pavilion provides Finnforest Merk with a unique showcase for Kerto, which has been engineered to give the Serpentine Pavilion its dramatic shape and structure.

Finnforest Merk is committed to innovative wooden architectural structures. While commonplace in Scandinavia and in other parts of Europe, large-scale architectural projects where the main structural material is timber are rarely seen in the UK.

Finnforest Merk is proud to be manufacturing and supplying all the bespoke Kerto elements of the structure and to work with Arup on delivering the engineering solution for the Serpentine Gallery Pavilion 2005. Together we have realised the architects' vision and created one of London's most visionary buildings.

John Tong
Managing Director
Finnforest UK

Member of Finnforest Corporation
MERK

# DIRECTOR'S
# FOREWORD

The Serpentine Pavilion 2005 is the result of a collaboration between Portugal's greatest living architect, the Pritzer Prize-winning Álvaro Siza, and his distinguished and innovative compatriot Eduardo Souto de Moura, best known for his 30,000-seat Braga Stadium. As in past years Cecil Balmond, Deputy Chairman of Arup, together with his team, has worked closely with Siza and Souto de Moura to develop the scheme.

Once again I am humbled and amazed by the generosity of the architects with whom we work, as well as their teams. We place them under what is sometimes intolerable pressure, but we have always been able to depend on their passion for the project to match ours. Bringing these pavilions into existence is a life-enhancing process, in which one genuinely feels a sense of 'one for all, and all for one', culminating in a structure of which we can be unconscionably proud. This year has been no exception and we are deeply indebted to the architects and their

colleagues, in particular Tiago Figueiredo, the endlessly patient lead architect, Tiago Coelho, Atsushi Ueno, their assistants Sandra Bastos and Anabela Monteiro, as well as to Siza's archivist, Chiara Porcu, who did so much to ensure the project's success.

Additionally, Siza not only generously designed chairs, stools, tables and chaises longues, elements that further enrich the experience of the structure, but he also gave his kind permission to make a limited-edition print from one of his initial drawings of the Pavilion. This sketch communicates his vision for the scheme, revealing the key characteristics of the building: the timber lattice structure, the canopy of solar-lights, and the way in which the polycarbonate cladding stops 1.3 m above the ground, affording seated visitors views of the surrounding park.

Cecil Balmond has been key to the Serpentine's Annual Architecture Commission since Arup's involvement in 2001. Not only has he guided his teams in every aspect of their work, but he was also involved in a design capacity in 2001, 2002 and, of course, this year. His understanding of the Gallery's ambition to present the work of leading international contemporary architects to the British public has enabled these projects to be realised. He is a valued colleague and friend.

His team at Arup developed the structural scheme for the building (using interlocking wooden beams arranged in a mutually supporting pattern with simple mortice-and-tenon connections), and then executed its design, detailing, fabrication and erection. Hamish Nevile, Lead Structural Designer, had previously worked on the Serpentine Gallery Pavilion 2003, and this experience proved crucial in enabling him to manage the design process. Martin Self, Structural Designer, analysed the structure and developed a project-specific script that exactly defined the individual geometries of the timber elements. Lip Chiong, Architectural Designer, helped to define the geometry of the building as well as developing many of the construction details in line with the architectural concept. Steve Walker provided the analysis and design input into the construction of the solar-lighting system. Charles Walker, who has worked on many of the previous pavilions, as Head of Advanced Geometry Unit, offered advice and

support. Our thanks also go to the members of the other team at Arup, who contributed their expertise: Andrew Hall, engineer in Facades, Anthony Ferguson engineer in Fire, and Timber materials specialist, Andrew Lawrence.

Peter Rogers, Managing Director, Stanhope plc, has been central to this project since 2001, when he first became involved with the Serpentine Gallery Pavilion, which was designed that year by Daniel Libeskind with Arup. His wise counsel and in-depth knowledge of construction and the industry has enabled us to steer the design and building of these structures with great confidence. Furthermore, he has actively involved in these projects his many associates in the business, championing the importance of contemporary architecture and thereby gathering support for the Serpentine's cause.

We are assisted in the rigorous selection of the architects by our advisors on the Board of Trustees, Lord Palumbo, Chairman, and Chairman of the Jury of the Pritzker Prize for Architecture, as well as Zaha Hadid, Trustee, and 2004 Pritzker Laureate, whose support is invaluable. Their involvement represents an important commitment by the Board to the strand in our programme devoted to architecture as well as to this exceptional project.

His Excellency Sr Fernando Andresen-Guimarães, Portuguese Ambassador, and Maria Elisa Domingues, Cultural Counsellor, Embassy of Portugal, have been generous with their time and suggestions, as well as being enthusiastic champions of the scheme. They were also instrumental in sourcing funding from the Instituto Camões, Portugal, for this publication.

Afassociados, consultants in engineering design and project management, and, in particular, Rui Furtado, Chief Executive Officer, as well as António Adão da Fonseca, President, and Raul Serafim, Associate, provided indispensable assistance as part of the Porto Architectural/Structural Liaison Team

João Fernandes, Director, Serralves Museum, and José Menezes, Press Officer, have proved gracious colleagues in a variety of different ways, including their generous hospitality and the provision of much information that greatly aided our endeavours.

Former Chief Executive of the Royal Parks, William Weston, Acting Chief Executive, Bernadette Kenny, and the current Chief Executive Mark Camley, together with their colleagues – Simon Betts and Nick Butler in particular – gave the project an encouraging early blessing, which made it possible for the Serpentine to progress the scheme with confidence.

We are grateful to many people at City of Westminster including Councillor Angela Hooper, Chairman of Planning and City Development Committee, Gordon Chard, Director of Planning and Transportation, Rosemarie MacQueen, Head of City Development, Gwyn Richards, Area Design and Conservation Area and Charles Vaton, District Surveyor, who gave us guidance on a variety of occasions both in the preparation and the realisation of the Pavilion. The project benefited significantly as a result and we highly value their support. We must also recognise the role played by Nick Fry, of the London Fire and Emergency Planning Authority in advising us on our safety strategy.

There was no budget for this project. It was a leap of faith on the part of the Trustees, the architects and ourselves. We are most thankful to Rudolf Ferscha, Chief Executive Officer, Eurex, who has generously committed his company's significant help over the years. He was inspired to make this pledge through an understanding of the pavilions' valuable contribution to the cultural landscape of London and beyond, as well as an empathy with the Serpentine's policy of access to

all. His vision has been matched by that of his colleague, Uwe Velten, Head of Marketing, Europe, who has worked hard to develop Eurex's association with the Serpentine.

This is the first Serpentine pavilion to have been built from wood and it would not have been possible without the sponsorship of leading timber experts Finnforest Merk. Enthusiasts of the scheme from the moment it was first presented to them, they have not only donated all of the material for the frame, but have also played a vital role in co-engineering it with Arup, as well as sourcing, fabricating and

erecting it, even extending their involvement to installing the polycarbonate cladding. Our sincerest thanks go to Ari Martonen, President and Chief Executive Officer, for the company's wholehearted engagement in the project, as well as to John Tong, Managing Director, and Warren Dudding, Marketing Manager. We are also most grateful to Michael Keller, European Project Manager, Jens Jamnitzky, Manager of European Research and Development and Technical Support, Josef Meier, Project Manager, and Jonathan Stone, Project Manager (UK), and their team on site, who ensured that the fabrication and construction of the frame

was completed to very high standards and with great speed and efficiency.

There are numerous other companies whose generosity has been central to the Pavilion's success. Their names make an impressive list, covering many different sectors of the construction industry, a number of whom have supported these architectural commissions in previous years. We are truly beholden to them because without their contribution it would have been impossible to achieve this project. Our heart-felt gratitude is extended to all those listed below:

**Platinum Sponsors**

Bovis Lend Lease Ltd, principal contractor and planning supervisor for the construction of the Pavilion, has advised the Serpentine Gallery and participated in every aspect of the scheme at each stage of its development. It has been a pleasure working with them and, in particular, Steven Evans, Divisional Director, Chris Pott, Project Manager, Stan Smith, Site Manager, Danny Ferry, Planning Supervisor, Danny Hine, Health and Safety and Keith Tang, Temporary Works.

Once again, David Hodgkiss, Chief Executive, Nick Day, Director, Gary Simmons, Associate

Director, and the team of Andy Thompson, Andy Bilinge and David Morris at William Hare have lent their considerable expertise in discussions concerning the structural steel design, as well as the fabrication and installation, in particular, the implementation of the steel ring beam foundations and the connection plates to brace the Pavilion's timber legs.

Ray O'Rourke, Chairman, Paul Collins, Managing Director at Laing O'Rourke, and their colleagues at Select Plant Hire supplied a crane and all the site equipment required for the erection of the Pavilion.

## Gold Sponsors

Chris Massie, Marketing Director, Clipfine Limited, provided overnight security and site support throughout the building of the Pavilion and the period of its opening to the public.

Richard Baldwin, Partner, and Paul Davis, Associate, of Davis Langdon, offered their skilled cost advice.

Barnaby Collins, Partner, DP9, submitted the Serpentine Gallery's planning application, advising on all issues connected to the process.

Stef Stefanou, Chairman, Eric Roberts, Regional Director, Mohammed Hurch, Site

Agent, and Simon Ford, Site Agent, John Doyle Group, organised and completed the ground works and provided site facilities.

Brendan Kerr, Managing Director, Keltbray Group, contributed on-site assistance and undertook to dismantle the Pavilion and remove all the foundations not associated with its re-use.

Serpentine Gallery Trustee, Marco Compagnoni, and his colleagues Jonathan Wood and Samantha McGonigle, Lovells, provided much-valued legal advice on a *pro bono* basis.

Shane Akeroyd, Managing Director, Genevieve Rooney, Vice President Marketing and Corina Blum Evans, Communications Manager, TD Securities, made a generous financial contribution to the Pavilion.

## Silver Sponsors

Richard Ford and Rupert Des Forges, Partners, Knight Frank, promoted the Pavilion to their many clients and successfully masterminded its sale.

Paola Bosso, Country General Manager, Barry Kitcher, Sales Director UK, David Rogers, Home Sales & Marketing Director, Claire

Rushworth, Category Marketing Manager, Alice Tan, Marketing Manager, Lavazza, are the first-time sponsors of the café.

Pat Stanborough, Chief Executive, and his team at T. Clarke plc, undertook the electrical installations.

## Bronze Sponsors
Arabella Lennox-Boyd, Director, and Emma Mazzullo, Practice Director, interpreted Siza's request for the re-landscaping of the Serpentine Gallery's existing lawn on the occasion of the Pavilion's erection.

John Gaffney, Managing Director, and Gavin Perry, Project Coordinator, SES Ltd, provided the site surveyors and engineers to set out the precise position of the Pavilion on the lawn.

Reidar Nesje, Commercial Director, Liz Richards, Senior Brand Manager, and Ashley Rolfe, Sales and Marketing Controller, Sikkens, provided colour to stain and treat the wood for the Pavilion's main timber structure.

We would like to take this opportunity to thank those contractors who have been especially helpful in ensuring the timely completion of the Pavilion: David Boughey of DB Construct, Martin

Bellamy, Senior Design Engineer, and Simon Gerard, Sales Manager of Solar Century, Michael Currell, Managing Director, Bay Plastics, and José Simões, S.Design, Portugal.

We would also like to acknowledge: Mark Hornsby for managing all audio aspects in the Pavilion; David Leister, Kino Club, for their projection services; Bob Pain, Director, Omni Colour Presentations Ltd, and Mark Jenkins, Director, K2 Screen Ltd, for the production of Siza's limited-edition print; Herman Lelie and Stefania Bonelli for their design and typesetting of the signage; as well as Mark Hix and Des McDonald of Rivington Grill, Bar and Deli for providing the catering service for the Pavilion café throughout the summer months; and Stevie Congdon, Managing Director, Lettice, for the catering at our opening celebrations.

Integral to the purpose of the Serpentine Pavilion is that it should constitute an exciting forum for learning and debate. *Time Out Park Nights at the Serpentine Gallery* includes a weekend of open-air film projections, shown on a 50-foot screen in Kensington Gardens, as well as Friday late-night architecture talks, film screenings, and sound events. *Time Out* has collaborated with the Serpentine in this programme and we are grateful to Tony Elliott, Founder and Chairman,

John Luck, Group Marketing Director, and Sandie Tozer, Magazine Brand Manager, Time Out Group Ltd, for appreciating from the outset the importance of the Pavilion to the cultural life of London during the summer months. Erica Bolton and Jane Quinn further enhanced the public's awareness through focusing the media's attention on this project.

We are also grateful to the many people who are involved in *Time Out Park Nights at the Serpentine Gallery* and our special thanks go to Paula Ridley, Director, and Miguel Santos, Director Anglo-Portuguese Cultural Relations at the Calouste Gulbenkian Foundation, who have very generously supported this programme. In addition we would like to acknowledge Ricky Burdett, who advised on the participants in the Architecture Talks; we are grateful both to him and to Jonathan Glancey for steering conversations with Álvaro Siza, Eduardo Souto de Moura, Cecil Balmond, Zaha Hadid, Hans Ulrich Obrist, Tony Fretton, Manuel Aires Mateus, Jamie Fobert, Manuel Graça Dias, Adam Caruso and Pedro Gadanho.

Our thanks also go to Lisa Le Feuvre, co-ordinator, Karen Alexander and Margaret

Deriaz, British Film Institute; the Park Sounds Committee: Rob Young, Anne Hilde Neset, Ed Baxter and Kaffe Matthews; the performers Paul Panhuysen, Steve Roden and Zeitkratzer: Reinhold Friedl, Burkhard Schlothauer, Anton Lukoszevieze, Ulrich Phillipp, Frank Gratkowski, Franz Hautzinger, Melvyn Poore, Marc Weiser, Maurice de Martin, Ralf Meinz and Andreas Harder.

Gigi Giannuzzi, Publisher, Trolley Books, has produced this publication, which has been designed by Martin Bell, with thanks to Anna Lopriore, and reveals and records the process of realising the Pavilion. We are greatly appreciative of their commitment. We are also most grateful to Hans Ulrich Obrist, Senior Curator, Musée d'Art Moderne de la Ville de Paris and Stefano Boeri, Editor, *Domus* for their introduction and interview with Cecil Balmond, and to Hans Ulrich Obrist for his interview with Álvaro Siza and Eduardo Souto de Moura, as well as to Edwin Heathcote for his extended captions. Ludwig Abache has once again photographically documented the Pavilion at the many stages of its construction and his images are included here, together with the distinguished work of Richard Bryant, as well as Tiago Figueiredo and Mark Robinson. Melissa Larner's editorial expertise

has been of inestimable benefit.

Mark Robinson, Project Manager, has worked on each Pavilion from 2000 to 2005 and none would have materialised without his knowledge and contribution in numerous ways. Each project has benefited immensely from his skill and experience and yet again we are truly indebted to him.

This year, Rebecca Morrill is the Project Organiser and she has masterminded the many administrative elements of the structure's realisation with great aplomb and efficiency. The entire Serpentine staff has been involved with this project, including the teams of Julie Burnell, Head of Building and Operations; Rose Dempsey, Head of Press; Natasha Harris, Head of Development; Louise Robson, Head of Finance; Sally Tallant, Head of Education Programming, as well as my hard-working assistant William Coggon.

The Council of the Serpentine is crucial to the Gallery's success and our manifold activities benefit hugely as a result of their commitment. Our enormous thanks to them, to the intrepid Summit Group, and to Richard and Ruth Rogers for their continuing engagement.

The Serpentine Gallery Pavilion is ambitious in the extreme. The many people mentioned here, as well as those who are not named but who still play an important role, are the reason why the project comes to fruition. Quite simply, it is due to them that this small miracle takes place and I cannot thank them enough.

Julia Peyton-Jones
Director
Serpentine Gallery

# FAST-FORWARD ARCHITECTURE
## JULIA PEYTON-JONES

There are probably many reasons why, in practical terms, we shouldn't commission contemporary architects to build a temporary pavilion at short notice in a Royal Park every year. There are probably many reasons why architects wouldn't want to do it and maybe about three reasons why they might agree to it. And if they were really to think about it, maybe only one.

The first question, then, must be why *do* we do it? Why does the Serpentine Gallery invite a renowned international architect to design a pavilion every year? And why do the architects agree? Why do we get involved in the stressful and costly process of construction? The reason is that we believe it to be the only way genuinely to expose people to the finest international contemporary architecture, the only way properly to display that architecture in a process that parallels the manner in which we commission and exhibit art.

Architecture exhibitions often have little to do with the actuality of architecture, frequently focusing on display and technology rather than on the buildings themselves. People need specialist knowledge in order to read plans, to unpick the computer-generated images, drawings, photographs, texts and models that constitute these exhibitions. So this kind of show tends to preach to the converted. In order to be really appreciated, architecture needs to be experienced first hand; the space must be felt, the colours seen, the textures engaged with. Being inside a building, absorbing the space, experiencing the light, is the only way to gain a true understanding of it.

Contemporary architecture can often be perceived as aloof or forbidding, obscure and exclusive. With the pavilion, however, we create something less intimidating, something bite-size, something that is temporary but that lingers in the imagination. It's our intention

Serpentine Gallery
Pavilion 2005
Designed by Álvaro Siza
and Eduardo Souto de
Moura with Cecil
Balmond – Arup

through the Pavilions to show people the extraordinary richness of contemporary architecture and allow them to compare their personal experience of one pavilion with the next, to become engaged and involved in the debate. There are no barriers or tickets sales. The public can simply walk in and take possession of the building.

If this sense of public ownership is one of the reasons why we do it, the next question must be, what, as a gallery, do we bring to the table, what do we do that's different from other commissioners?

The answer is that what we do at the Serpentine is to display objects, and we see the pavilion as a super-sized object. We bring the model of working with artists, of commissioning, collaborating, enabling, encouraging, translating, facilitating, shaping and guiding, to the process of working with architects. We set out to achieve their vision. The art world has a very different way of doing things from that of the construction world. Artists don't wait for a client to commission their work – they create it using the tools and the resources that are available at the time. There's no better example of this spirit than the *Freeze* show of 1988, which did so much to establish Young British Artists in the media and in the public eye. Here,

Richard Serra
*Serpentine Corner* 1992
2 parts 1.67 x 5.74 m
Installation at
Serpentine Gallery
© 2005 Richard Serra

the artists organised the show themselves, renting an empty warehouse and arranging taxis to encourage influential members of the art world to attend. This inspirational paradigm catapulted the world of visual art out of complacency and into action. And it is against this background that it has been possible to engage public interest and promote awareness of the visual arts. The greatly improved climate and openness to new art has enabled the Serpentine Gallery to embrace architecture as part of its programme. And the radical shift in the media, which now features contemporary design in its many different forms – a far cry from the fashion for pine furniture and the celebration of all things historical in previous decades – has also facilitated this new atmosphere of tolerance and experimentation.

The Serpentine Programme has always welcomed interventions in the actual structure of the building in order to alter the perception of the Gallery and its surroundings. We promote a continual reinterpretation of the spaces within the Gallery and the park in which it sits. In 1992, for example, Richard Serra was commissioned to make concurrent interventions at the Serpentine and at Tate. For the Serpentine he demonstrated his sophisticated understanding of space through an installation of drawings that he made *in situ*. He said of his Serpentine show:

> The installation could either reinforce the symmetry of the building or point to differences between similar spaces. We could take down all later additions and reveal the original architectural function, which was that of a refreshment pavilion in Kensington Gardens. But why change the character of the Serpentine to something that it originally was, when its specific function, now, is to show works of art? To delve into the archaeology of the site as a method to reassert or to critique its present function is not relevant to me. The content of the

drawing installations does not reside in the process of their making, nor does it reside in the delineation of the field of a black canvas. The content resides in the viewer's experience of the space and place as it is redefined through the installation. For example, two black canvasses on walls opposite each other compress and redefine the physical volume of the space and weight of the room.

Richard Wilson's exhibition *Jamming Gears* in 1996 was the last show at the Serpentine prior to its renovation. It played with the concept of the Gallery as a building site, and incorporated

Richard Wilson
*Jamming Gears* 1996
Installation at
Serpentine Gallery
© 2005
Richard Wilson

much of the equipment that would later be used in the construction, including forklift trucks, building-site huts, bore holes, as well as necessitating the digging of a large rectangular pit. The project punctured the fabric of the Gallery, exposing hidden spaces and revealing the fragility of the structure – it became obvious that the building had no foundations. The impact of the objects that Wilson placed in and through the Gallery created an unnerving clash of cultures.

Doug Aitken's *New Ocean* in 2001 allowed us to stretch our ideas of how the Gallery could be used. The lantern on the roof was turned into a lighthouse, while the entrance was through a small, nondescript door in the lobby that led to the usually off-limits basement, our workshop and store, where newly-commissioned video works were shown. From there, visitors went up a specially-made staircase to pop, like the white rabbit, out of a hatch in the Gallery floor. The Serpentine's architecture was subverted and disrupted by Aitken's total intervention, which quite literally turned peoples' experience of the building inside out and upside down.

The Architecture Programme is an extension of the way in which we commission work for the Gallery. We invite the architects with whom we want to collaborate, and in effect we sit round the kitchen table to work things out. The discussions with them and their teams are direct, and every aspect of the project is transparent, making for an extremely engaging and enjoyable process. We don't set up a competition to select the architects, as would usually be the case with such projects, because the decision is a curatorial one. However, the Pavilion is resolutely a commission for architects, not artists. Furthermore, only international architects who have not completed a building in the UK at the time of our invitation are eligible, since the aim is to introduce the public to the work of international practitioners; British architects may be well represented abroad, but foreign architects remain under-represented here.

If the *Freeze* show was the inspiration that showed us what could be achieved, it was the renovation of our own Gallery that spurred us into thinking about the commissioning of architects. When the Serpentine asked John Miller and Partners to work on the feasibility study to renovate the Gallery, the function of the Serpentine as a site for the presentation of art was of primary importance; the building took second place. The brief focused on the adaptability of the galleries, and putting in place all the

Doug Aitken
*New Ocean* 2001
Installation at
Serpentine Gallery
© 2005 Doug
Aitken

necessary requirements for the showing of modern and contemporary art, as well as anticipating what artists would need in the twenty-first century. It was necessary to use every bit of space as efficiently as possible, since the restrictions of the 1934 Grade II listed building and our Royal Parks landlords prevented us from expanding. John Miller and I had numerous conversations about trying to fit a quart into a pint pot in terms of what we wanted the building to accommodate, and his solution to this challenge was elegant, adaptable and eminently useable. (It accommodates 590,000 people a year, and up to 4,500 in a day.)

Around the time of the renovation, we presented a range of commissions, which culminated in Tadashi Kawamata's work. Somewhat prosaically called *Relocation Project for the Serpentine Gallery Lawn*, it took place concurrently with a show at Annely Juda Fine Art, in 1997. He observed that both galleries have in common the character of daylight that fills their exhibition spaces, and of the Serpentine he said, 'By using some of the glass doors and windows of the old Serpentine Gallery together with recycled and other timber I was able to build a structure that replicates the Serpentine on the Gallery lawn just before the new, renovated galleries are completed.'

The renovation was run on a construction-management basis, a process that kept us at arm's length from the architects. It was the antithesis of how we work as a Gallery with artists, which is collaboratively, in a manner that facilitates, encourages and enables. The project was late and lacking in teamwork – the construction management process patently did not deliver what it promised. Furthermore, it underscored our powerlessness as the client. However, it taught us many lessons that we put to good use in the annual architecture commission. Because we're independent of the architectural world, unfamiliar with its rules, we have the freedom to devise our own way of doing things,

with the benefit of the best specialist advice. We use the model that informs all our work in the organisation of our Exhibition Programme. What's been so fascinating about our experience with the pavilions is that it is such a benign process, the diametric opposite of the blame culture that appears to exist in the construction process. It relies on the generosity of all involved and only works because everyone has to take a leap of faith.

The Serpentine Gallery has contributed, together with its larger and smaller colleagues in the public and private sector, to making London a

Tadashi Kawamata
*Relocation Project for the Serpentine Gallery Lawn* 1997
© 2005 Tadashi Kawamata

centre of the contemporary art world, a position for this city that would have seemed inconceivable only fifteen years ago. This has been achieved in spite of a paucity in public funding, by co-opting the creativity and harnessing the dynamism that has elevated the contemporary visual arts to this position. It has been a combination of educating the public, gathering the energy and passionately creating the culture fostered by the *Freeze* exhibition, which showed that if the system doesn't work, you can invent your own. It is exactly this DIY ethic that has inspired us and it is my avowed opinion that anyone can do it.

If the idea of the pavilions is to exhibit architecture through creating, rather than curating it, the question arises: what exactly is it that we're creating? We don't do it to gain publicity, or even to provide a café for the summer. The point is simply to display first-class architecture to the public.

The brief for the pavilion specifies, among others, that it should be 'a functioning example of the architect's work'. It is a temporary pavilion and one that embodies the possibility of being designed as a demountable structure that could be sold on or even rolled out as an edition or multiple.

The first pavilion in 2000 was designed by Zaha Hadid for the Serpentine's thirtieth anniversary. The £100,000 budget was effectively no more than the cost of hiring a big tent, dressing it and filling it with flowers. Hadid responded with something that was principally a container, for which she also designed the furniture. Chris Smith, then Secretary of State for Culture, Media and Sport, liked the pavilion so much that he granted it an extension to its original three-day installation so that it could stay up throughout the summer. We quickly installed a café, and the model for what we were to do in the following years was born. It was the genesis of the pavilion idea, the prototype, and it proved that we could do it. Hadid's work stood for everything that I admired and wanted to emulate in subsequent projects. Hers was a resolutely international sensibility although she had never built anything permanent in this country.

Her pavilion employed the architectural language of the canopy: the roof folded and dipped in a series of angular moves, while the structure of the building was made up of props and struts. The result was appropriately summery and gave a fascinating glimpse of Hadid's constructivist, graphic style of geometric form and angular planes. Of it, she wrote:

The design was to create a tent typology, which, via a triangulated roof, seeks to play with the traditional notion of a tensile fabric construction. Whilst it maintains the sense of ephemerality, its folding form of angular, flat planes subverts the lightness of the fabric by giving it an illusion of solidity.
The nature of the folding planes engages with the site by extending itself to the ground at points whilst at the same time undulating to create a variety of internal spaces. These undulations are further exploited by the positioning of lighting between the two roof fabrics, which incurs gradual changes over time by shifting contrast through the roof planes. The internal ground plane is occupied by a field of specially-designed tables, which create a movement through the space where their colour graduates from white to black, reinforcing a sense of movement dissipating through the tent.

Hadid's important contribution to the Serpentine continues as a Trustee and an advisor to the Annual Architecture Commission. However, our greatest debt to her is for putting us on the path of working with architects on an ongoing basis.

The following year Daniel Libeskind was invited to design the pavilion. His studio works in exactly the same way as we do at the Serpentine.

Serpentine Gallery Pavilion 2001 *Eighteen Turns* Designed by Daniel Libeskind with Arup

His team embraced the project and the time-scale with relish. The whole project was completed from start to finish, including planning, in four months, even though they were working on the Imperial War Museum North at the same time. One of the many significant things to come out of this project was the introduction to Libeskind's long-term friend and collaborator, Cecil Balmond, of the structural

engineering firm Arup, with whom we've worked ever since. This was also the year in which we met Peter Rogers, Managing Director of Stanhope plc and our Project Advisor, who keeps an eye on everything to do with the construction.

Libeskind's building too, entitled *Eighteen Turns*, proved to be the first he completed in the UK and, like Hadid's, his structure was an exploration of folding techniques, perhaps the most eloquent exposition of his collapsing structural and spatial design. He was interested in an origami-like process of folding panels spiralling around to meet themselves at their own beginning. It was a simplified version of the Victoria & Albert Museum design, the *Spiral*, and foreshadowed the forms of his later proposal for the replacement of the World Trade Center, which would be destroyed a few months after the Serpentine's Pavilion rose up.

'Each of the four interlocking sections of the structure is made from three panels attached to the floor base to form a complete unit', Libeskind explained:

> The first panel rises from ground level, forming a natural arch and 'folds' into the next section, which 'folds' into the next, until the final arch and last panel return to the ground level. The structure, with walls, floor and roof, creates a continuous spiral that moves across the ground creating labyrinths and viewing panels from within the structure.'

Toyo Ito's pavilion followed Libeskind's in 2002. Like its predecessor, it was a collaboration in design terms with Cecil Balmond. Essentially an exploration of the columnless box, it was an algorithmic structure made up of lines crossing in space, a visual puzzle that pushed the eye around its form. The whole concept of the permeable, temporary structure appealed to Ito's fondness for lightness and ethereality:

> There is something very attractive about the idea of it existing only temporarily for three months. Whereas just the thought that the buildings I design might stand for a hundred years or more wears heavily on me, the notion of a temporary project is liberating in many ways. One need not be so strict about function nor worry about how it will age. And it seems to me, it just might offer the clearest expression of the concepts I habitually imagine.

Thus the pavilion's temporality and the extremely fast programme can provoke architects into experimentation. As well as being encapsulations of their creators' oeuvres, the pavilions can also act as a significant spur to the expansion of their ideas, while conventional buildings can often stifle ambition. The pavilion can be the embodiment of the dynamism of an architect's sketch, the most direct realisation of the mythical drawing on the napkin or the back of an envelope.

Ito concluded that the pavilion was 'a curious art object that is clearly architecture, yet at the same time non-architecture. The reason being that, while offering the bare minimum of functions as a space for people's activities, it on the other hand has no columns, no windows, no doors – that is, it has none of the usual architectural elements.'

The great Brazilian architect Oscar Niemeyer, whose pavilion followed Ito's in 2003, was acutely conscious of the brief to embody his extraordinary oeuvre in a single structure. This was surely the only opportunity that British audiences would have to encounter his work first hand on their own soil.

He wrote: My purpose in designing the Pavilion for the Serpentine Gallery in Hyde Park was to express what I think are the main characteristics of my architecture through a simple and small-scale work. Thus, by suspending the weight of the Pavilion one and a half metres above the ground, I was able to achieve its distinctive

lightness. At the same time I wanted to give the profile of the Pavilion a dynamic line, since it is with this play of curves and straight lines that I produce my architecture. My other objective was to achieve simplicity and good use of colours and coverings, so that the interiors could achieve the unity required of any work of architecture.

Niemeyer included a number of elements that he saw as characteristic of his oeuvre: the red ramp, the distinctive roof profile (which emerged in the very first meeting we had), a semi-submerged auditorium, and a grand staircase. Among his principal problems was that, almost more than any architect alive, he is known for his concrete constructions. Here he had to design an essentially lightweight structure, a demountable pavilion. He initially refused the commission, saying 'I only use concrete, and I design permanent buildings', but ultimately he agreed. When asked why, he replied, 'possibly because it is a type of construction that is so very different. I'm happy to have done it.' The final Pavilion, a steel-framed structure clad in aluminium, achieved the desired result. It was José Carlos Sussekind, Niemeyer's engineer and long-standing friend and collaborator for thirty

years, who referred to it as 'a project that performs the miracle of "monumentality" on a very small scale.' Rowan Moore wrote evocatively in the *Evening Standard*: 'Imagine Garbo or Sinatra in their prime and performing now. With this week's opening of the 2003 Serpentine Gallery Pavilion, just such a time-warping miracle is taking place.' Niemeyer included the Pavilion as one of a small number of projects in the special exhibition devoted to his work in the São Paolo Biennial of Architecture and Design of the same year.

The semi-submerged auditorium in concrete was integral to Niemeyer's design and it was our job to build it. There were a few mutterings about it seeming more like a permanent building than a pavilion, but this lower level was key to Niemeyer's concept. If we encourage architects to push the boundaries, then we have a duty to match them in their ambition. In any case, the auditorium was only a hole in the ground, just like the one Richard Wilson had made in the Gallery itself for his exhibition. This is what architects and artists should do: challenge the institution, test our ability to respond, and create what they feel to be right.

If Niemeyer's pavilion attempted minuscule monumentality, the subsequent design in 2004,

by the radical Dutch practice MVRDV, addressed it on a much larger scale. The idea was to cover the Gallery itself in a faux mountain structure. After Niemeyer, we had deliberately approached a younger practice to create a balance in the annual programme. More experimental and with an entirely different working practice, MVRDV seemed an interesting counterpoint. Just as Niemeyer's roof profile had emerged at the very beginning, so MVRDV's idea for the mountain was there from the outset. Obviously there is more than a hint of dry humour in the notion of a practice from the Netherlands, the flattest country in Europe, proposing a mountain in the park. And indeed their idea was exceptionally

radical. Against all the odds, we managed to secure the in-principle permissions necessary. However, it proved to be a project that tested us on every level: its budget, as slippery as a snake, refused to be pinned down. It also pushed us in terms of time, materials, expertise and logistics. But how could we not have tried to build it on seeing the first extraordinary images?

The Trustees wholeheartedly supported the project and I wrestled with the challenges, along with my compatriot-in-arms on all the pavilions, Mark Robinson, the Project Manager. Of all the proposals it is this one, which is still in development, that has forced the most complete re-interpretation of the built and spatial form of the Gallery. It's also the only one that has proved too ambitious, for the moment. Yet it is no less a project than any of those completed.

In complete contrast, the current year's pavilion has been designed by Álvaro Siza and Eduardo Souto de Moura, along with Cecil Balmond. It involves – as usual – the latter's team at Arup, this year liaising with the architects' long-term Portuguese colleagues at Afassociados, consultants in engineering design and project management. Despite successful forays into grandiosity with their Portuguese Pavilion at the 1998 Lisbon Expo and Souto de Moura's astonishing football stadium at Braga for the 2004 European Championships, neither architect is known for monumentality. Quite to the contrary, both are internationally respected for their subtlety, wit and sublime delicacy, and the inventiveness with which they apply it to the small scale, to the everyday.

Their design was a surprise; the pavilion is constructed of an undulating, organic timber grid. Siza describes it:

> like an animal whose legs are firmly attached to the ground, but whose body is tense from hunger, with an arched back and taut skin.

With its head lowered and limbs locked, it remains rooted to the spot, but poised for movement – almost as if the Serpentine itself might be consumed ...
The key objective was to avoid creating an isolated and anonymous pavilion and instead to guarantee that the new building – while presenting a totally different architecture – establishes a 'dialogue' with the Neo-classical building.

The sensual grid (an irony in itself) undulates 130 centimetres above the lawn, giving the effect of a floating structure but one with the visual and physical permeability of a marquee roof. The building is anchored to the ground by a carpet of grey bricks, which provides a hard floor surface. This is a project about negative space and absence. It sits in a bowl like a lurking reptile. The scheme is the first to have focused on the grounds around the Pavilion, which have been gently re-landscaped for the occasion.

This pavilion embodies the temporary, fleeting nature of this project in the park. When I asked Siza for his views on making a demountable structure that would be sited elsewhere when subsequently purchased by a new owner, he responded:

The pavilion is no different from a permanent building. It has a short life at the Serpentine. Therefore, the design requires more care when it is *in situ* for such a short time. It is difficult to achieve the right solution for this site and the fact that it is visible for such a short time means that its legacy must remain in one's memory, or in photographs.

Part of the thrill of building the pavilions is the idea that the particular conditions of this project have pushed the architects to create something new. As Balmond has said:

> The Serpentine Pavilion each year gives the opportunity for a small structure to be built without the demands of a complex brief, allowing the chance for experiment and the pushing of boundaries. Structure, form and architecture become the same thing in these projects due to the close collaboration between engineer and architect. It also allows for the exploration of an engineering aesthetic in the solution.

The lack of a complex brief is one of the key characteristics of the project. The pavilion is in essence a container that need not contain. The structure itself has no services to speak of and as a result it allows architects, like the artists in the Exhibition Programme whom we commission, to push the boundaries of their work. It is this that really makes our annual architecture commission unique.

The pavilion's use as a café is an important consideration in so far as it gives visitors a purpose, so that they feel no awkwardness about spending time in the space. In this way the architecture almost creeps up on them and they can unselfconsciously experience fine examples of work by some of the leading international architects of today.

The Serpentine has no budget for the pavilions, which makes it all the more remarkable that the Gallery in December 2004 was placed number fourteen in *RIBA Journal's* list of top fifty UK clients, a chart that commends clients who aspire to high quality design and are prepared to take calculated risks. The cost of the pavilions ranges from £100,000 to £1.2 million, excluding fees. But it is worth noting that even our most expensive annual commission is comparable in cost to major international block-buster exhibitions, which are also temporary projects that leave nothing except memories, a catalogue and a smattering of postcards.

The Serpentine does not pay a fraction of these costs – if we did, the commission would be untenable, since we must also raise an annual £2.2 million for the rest of our work, while retaining free admission. Fundraising is therefore essential and we collaborate with an impressive list of extraordinarily generous companies and individuals, to whom we are truly indebted.

When we were renovating the Serpentine, it was impossible to elicit the help of the construction industry. In the main, contemporary architecture has not seemed to be something that is of compelling interest to the owners and managing directors of these companies. But now they play an important role in making the pavilions happen.

So does this eschew the idea that in general it is impossible to do things without money? My own view is that if the idea is good enough and the will is there then everything else will follow even the sale of the pavilion – which contributes 40 percent of the budget – by the estate agents, Knight Frank. They market the structure in exactly the same way as they do the great country houses that they also sell. This marketing by the establishment to the establishment of an art form not embraced by the establishment seems enjoyably subversive.

The money is raised for the Pavilion against the scheme as soon as it is known and everything proceeds from there. The architects are invited in November, the first meeting is in December, the design finished in February or March, by which time it will have been costed and companies already approached for sponsorship. In the case of this year's pavilion, there was only one company in Europe that could have made the structure, and in time. To their great credit, Finnforest Merk not only said yes but agreed to sponsor the timber element entirely.

So to return to my question at the outset: why are architects keen to accept the commission of designing our pavilions? The answer is, possibly because it's an irresistible idea. As Ito says: 'The project is liberating in many ways'. And why do we do it? Because our flexibility and the way in which we are used to working means that we are able to deliver a direct experience of structures designed by some of the finest contemporary architects to a public and a press that has been extraordinarily receptive. The Pavilion Programme not only introduces a broad range of people to contemporary architecture but also raises the bar for exciting building in the UK.

*This is an edited version of the RIBA Trust's Annual Lecture given by Julia Peyton-Jones on 21 April 2005, RIBA, London.*

# ÁLVARO SIZA
# SELECTED PROJECTS

**CARLOS BEIRES HOUSE,
PÓVOA DE VARZIM,
PORTUGAL, 1973–76**

In this project Siza constructed
a box, only to break it open.
It is nicknamed the 'Bomb
house' because one corner
has been deliberately
destroyed, partly in response
to Siza's dissatisfaction with
the design standard of the
surrounding houses. It has
been replaced with a glass
membrane, which opens out
the rooms onto an internal
courtyard, almost like a series
of verandahs. 'Mysteriously',
the architect writes, 'this
house was built, and to the
client's satisfaction.'
Edwin Heathcote

## QUINTA DA MALAGUEIRA, SOCIAL HOUSING, ÉVORA, PORTUGAL, 1977–95

This large social housing scheme was intended for people who had migrated from the countryside. It deliberately avoids an overtly urban approach but at the same time retains urban elements – the density, the internal streets, the intimation of gates. Siza has developed a familiar language of white blocks and walls and inward-looking houses that seems to refer to Moorish as well as to local vernacular traditions. The scheme can be compared to the humane and wonderful works of Hassan Fathy in Egypt in its attempt to reconcile a modern language with a recognisable local identity as an architecture for the poor. EH

## APARTMENT BUILDING, SCHLESISCHES TOR, KREUZBERG, BERLIN, GERMANY, 1980–84

While the architect Aldo Rossi and other postmodernists were creating monumental urban facades in Berlin using fragments of the classical or deconstructed city, Siza simply wrapped his apartments in an undulating veneer of render. The scale and repetitive grid picks up on the surrounding historic blocks, while the curves recall the Expressionism of Erich Mendelsohn et al that briefly flourished in the city in the 1920s. Less subtle and inventive than the best of his Portuguese work, this apartment block was nevertheless the first to expose Siza to an international audience.  EH

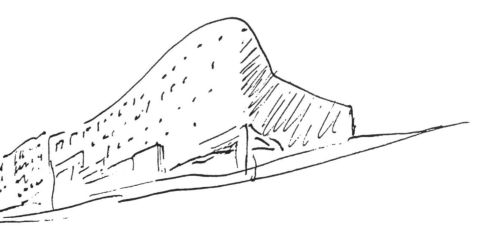

## CARLOS RAMOS PAVILION, FACULTY OF ARCHITECTURE, PORTO, PORTUGAL, 1985–86

In this building Siza unites the modernist traditions of Bauhaus functionalism (Walter Gropius, Mies van der Rohe, Le Corbusier) with Organic modernism (Hans Scharoun, Erich Mendelsohn, Alvar Aalto) and slots them effortlessly into both the Porto streetscape and a contemporary idiom. Austere elevations relieved by strip windows and occasional sculptural massing give on to rich interiors and a library in which the dramatic skylight spine sucks light down into the pages of the books on the desks. EH

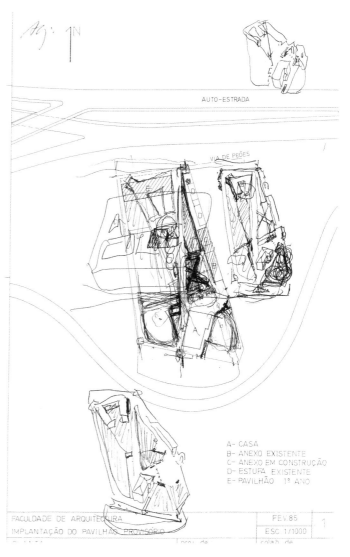

AUTO-ESTRADA

VIA DE PEÕES

A- CASA
B- ANEXO EXISTENTE
C- ANEXO EM CONSTRUÇÃO
D- ESTUFA EXISTENTE
E- PAVILHÃO 1º ANO

FACULDADE DE ARQUITECTURA
IMPLANTAÇÃO DO PAVILHÃO PROVISÓRIO

FEV.85
ESC.1/1000

1

## MUSEUM OF CONTEMPORARY ART, SERRALVES FOUNDATION, PORTO, PORTUGAL, 1991–99

Set in the grounds of an Art Deco mansion, the Serralves Museum takes the visitor on a carefully constructed journey through a series of exquisite architectural moments and unexpected details. The galleries seem simple, allowing the exhibits full rein, but at their edges they are deceptively complex, always attracting a delicate light and affording carefully framed views of the exterior landscape.  EH

## PORTUGUESE PAVILION FOR EXPO '98, LISBON, PORTUGAL, 1995–98
## ÁLVARO SIZA AND EDUARDO SOUTO DE MOURA WITH CECIL BALMOND – ARUP

This unusual, seemingly oxymoronic building of lightweight monumentalism, which brought Siza his biggest audience, is curiously uncharacteristic. There is a hint of Rossi, of Giorgio de Chirico, even of Italian Fascist architecture in the tall, deep arcades, but it is leavened by the lightness of the huge span of the concrete canopy, which is gently draped between the pavilion buildings, defining a wonderful and generous public space.  EH

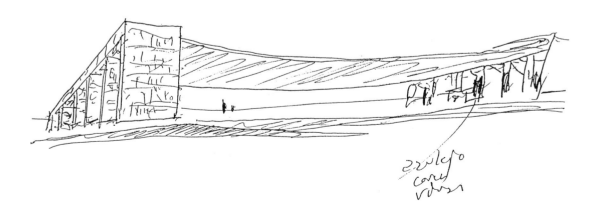

## PORTUGUESE PAVILION FOR EXPO 2000, HANOVER, GERMANY, 1999–2000
## ÁLVARO SIZA AND EDUARDO SOUTO DE MOURA WITH CECIL BALMOND – ARUP

This seemingly conventional and typically serious piece of Mediterranean modernism is leavened by its weird, undulating roof, as if the sober envelope is barely able to contain the excitement of what is on the inside. Given that they are the country's best-known and most widely respected architects, the choice of Siza and Souto de Moura for the national pavilion seems entirely natural, but there is something incongruous, about Siza in particular – an architect who excels in the field of the everyday and the finely wrought detail – becoming involved in such an obviously bombastic showpiece in what is effectively a theme-park setting. Nevertheless, as they have shown at the Lisbon and Hanover Expos and now at the Serpentine Gallery, both architects have become adept at using even the most fleeting of contexts to say something interesting and surprising about form, and about the nature of public space and architecture itself.  EH

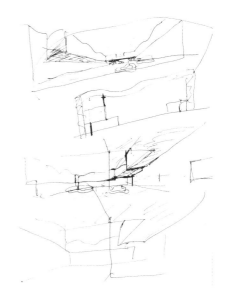

# EDUARDO SOUTO DE MOURA
## SELECTED PROJECTS

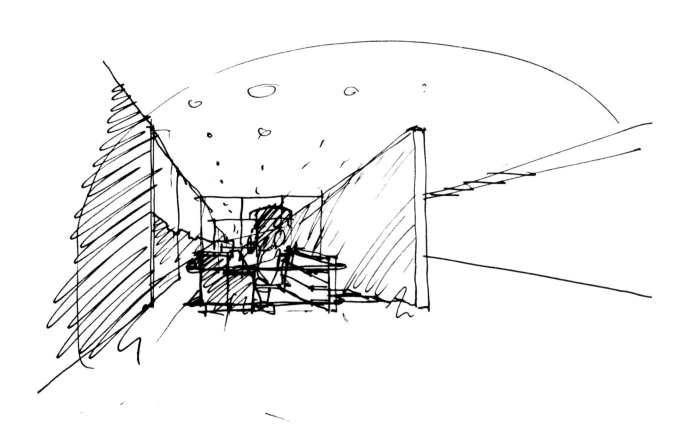

## CASA DAS ARTES,
## CULTURAL CENTRE, S.E.C.,
## PORTO, PORTUGAL, 1981–91

'I want the building to remain anonymous, which is the opposite of going unnoticed', said Souto de Moura about this arts centre, which takes its cue from the stone of the park in which it sits. Internal walls are of concrete but treated like partitions, only touching the floor on slender legs, which allows the spaces to flow through the building. Natural illumination is achieved through skylights, the deep reveal intimating the massive presence of a roof pushing down on the spaces to emphasise the length of the galleries and cinema. Jacques Herzog (of Herzog and de Meuron) has identified the architect's work as being all about a wall. This structure, with its overshooting spine wall governing the simple spaces around it, demonstrates his point with great clarity.  EH

## POUSADA SANTA MARIA DO BOURO, AMARES, PORTUGAL, 1989-97

The masterly conversion of this old monastery building into a Pousada, or hotel, eloquently demonstrates Souto de Moura's delicate touch with history and particularly with stone. Nothing in the new architecture overpowers the solid historic fabric, yet every detail appears as a revelation; every deft intervention serves to accentuate a view, an old detail, or merely the changing light between a room and a courtyard.  EH

## CASA DA MUSICA METRO STATION, PORTO, PORTUGAL, 1997–2005

An antidote to Rem Koolhaas's huge Casa da Musica above it, the metro station is composed of a pair of canopies bridging two massive concrete drums. Serene and understated, it exudes a calm, rational control, which is the mark of all Souto de Moura's subterranean and surface metro stations. These are beginning to exert a real impact on a city that is more conscious than most of the importance of its architects.  EH

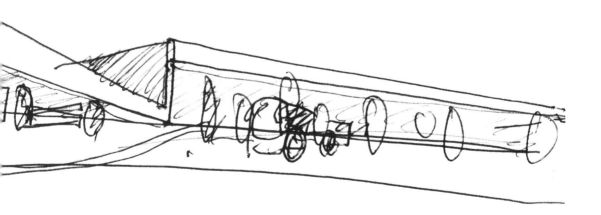

## CINEMA HOUSE FOR MANOEL DE OLIVEIRA, PORTO, PORTUGAL, 1998–2003

An unusually sculptural piece sees Souto de Moura moving away from his characteristic blend of stone spine and glass walls with a structure in which the edges of the internal spaces are presented as open-ended boxes, a counter to the building's hemmed-in-on-all-sides situation. The architect refers to these two huge openings as the building's 'eyes'. He previously experimented with this anthropomorphic approach in a house on the Rua do Crasto, Porto, (1996–2001), in which windows are conceived as eyes and nose and the entrance as a great timber-clad maw.  EH

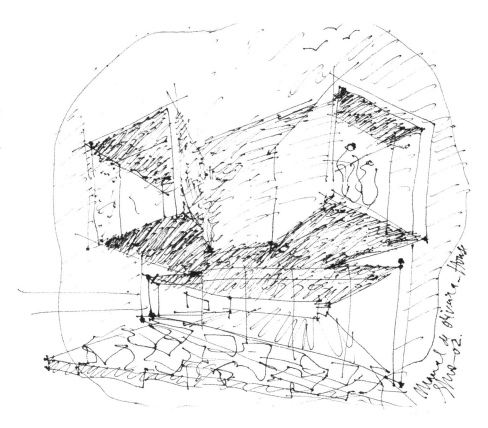

## BRAGA STADIUM, BRAGA, PORTUGAL, 1999–2003

A natural extension of Souto de Moura's long love affair with stone is his placing of a building in a quarry. Perhaps the most dramatic stadium since Frei Otto's Olympic Stadium in Munich (1972), the theatrical concrete terraces face each other, whilst the ground to one side forms a natural amphitheatre and to the other falls away to give a view onto the town below. The two stands, which appear to be casually leaning back, are bound together by steel cables. Not only do they perform a structural function, but they also imply a covering over the pitch, defining the space below. Because they are to either side of the pitch with nothing behind the goals, all spectators are privileged in their view and the stadium becomes a part of the mountainside rather than something imposed upon it. The rocks are allowed to peep through the concrete at points, so that one is always aware of the power of the rock, as if the stadium could be gradually subsumed into the landscape. Dramatic and pantheistic, this is as close as one can get to the Greek amphitheatre in the landscape, even if its antecedents are reportedly the rope bridges and stone terraces of the Incas.  EH

## TWO HOUSES, FOMELOS, PONTE DE LIMA, 2001–02

'Ever since my first project, I have gone on designing the same house, as if obsessed', explains Souto de Moura. Here, one house cantilevers grandly over the sloping landscape, whilst the other appears to be tumbling down it at a worrying angle. This extraordinary project embodies both sophisticated structural engineering, and the slightly subversive sense of humour that Souto de Moura often allows to peep through in his work.  EH

entrada

# CECIL BALMOND
# SELECTED PROJECTS

## MAISON A FLOIRAC, BORDEAUX, AQUITAINE, FRANCE, 1994–98
### ARCHITECT: OMA/REM KOOLHAAS

Photograph: The house floats over the city of
Bordeaux, a powerful mass of levitating concrete,
held by offset columns and a slender tie into the
ground; it is a vanishing act of sorts, of gravity
being denied direct support.

Sketch: The response to supporting a weight
up in the air is to have props directly below it.
In the Bordeaux Villa, columns migrate outside
the footprint, and one of them turns into a tie.
The result is an extreme condition of balance.
Cecil Balmond

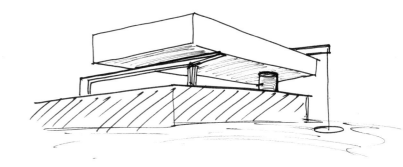

## PORTUGUESE NATIONAL PAVILION EXPO '98, LISBON, PORTUGAL, 1995–98

ÁLVARO SIZA AND EDUARDO SOUTO DE MOURA

Photograph: It is not just a bird that flies, the air allows an intersection. We may know that an outspread wing on a thermal current supports the moment of falling to overcome the wrench of gravity, but such an effortless sweep creates a paradox. Where there was nothing the flight leaves a memory. Shape and volume come to the surrounding space, an action of the positive drawing out a hidden negative.

Sketch: A weight hanging in the air like beads on a necklace – the 'string' attachment to the end abutments, 'loosening' the structure to 'bounce' should an earthquake hit Lisbon. CB

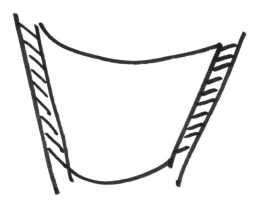

**SEATTLE CENTRAL LIBRARY, SEATTLE,
WASHINGTON, USA, 1999–2003
ARCHITECTS:** OMA/LMN ARCHITECTS.

**Photograph:** The diamond-patterned mesh
offers seismic resistance to earthquakes, not
only an attractive skin but a medium of flow for
a structural binding action.
**Sketch:** A series of boxes slide past each other
and house the program for library and
administration facilities. A stressed skin wraps
around the displacement to offer protection
against seismic action. CB

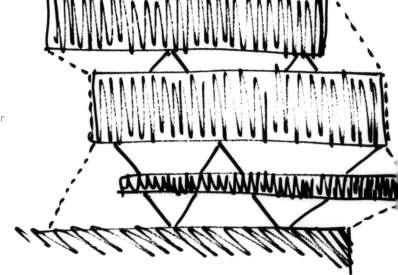

**ANISH KAPOOR, *MARSYAS* 2002-03**
**TATE MODERN, LONDON, UK**

Photograph: The thin fabric of just over 1 mm flies 140 m in length and soars up to 35 m in the Tate Modern, a manifold, undulating, – its name "Marsyas" – acting more as an armature and internal prop to the volume of the building rather than serving as a piece of sculpture within it.

Sketch: Three rings provide the shaping function to a membrane that is pulled tight between them. The fabric is tailored so that under tension there is a top catenary curvature and at the lower half two arching shapes.  CB

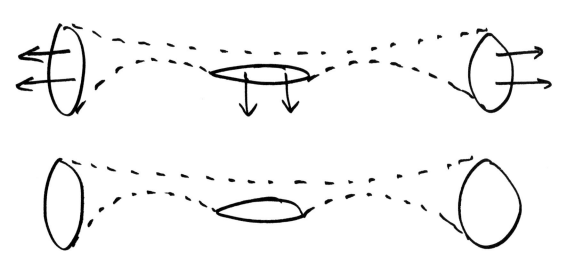

**CHINA CENTRAL TELEVISION (CCTV)
HEADQUARTERS, BEIJING,
CHINA, 2003-08
ARCHITECTS:** OMA/REM KOOLHAAS,
OLE SCHEEREN

Photograph: CCTV comprises half a million
square metres of broadcasting facilities
and offices in Beijing for China Central
Television.  The building rises 240 m and
cranks in the air, coming down the other
side in a gigantic loop. The bracing pattern
is serial, and changing density as shown
on the façade, following the stresses as
they vary over the face of the building.
Sketch: Bracing pattern that is noded
correctly, intersecting floors and columns,
but when the supporting framework of
columns and beams is removed, and only
the bracing revealed, the pattern has
variable dimensions and broken, abrupt,
endings.  CB

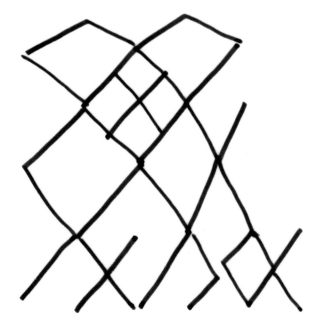

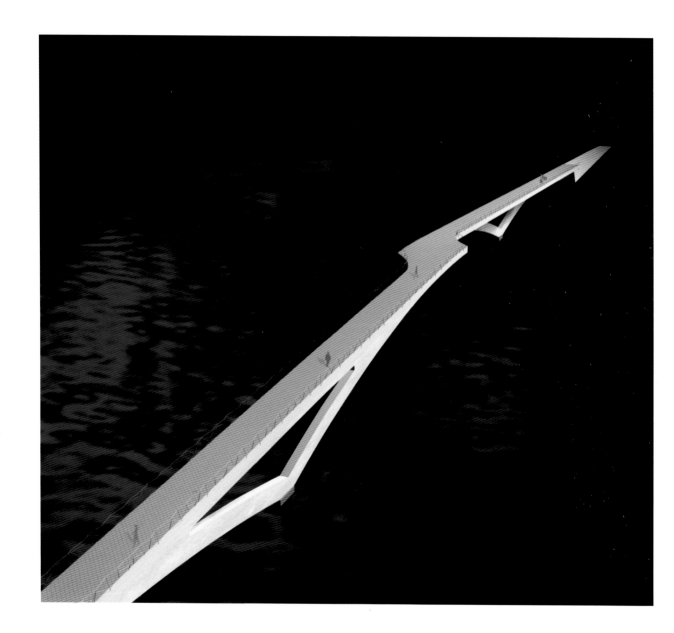

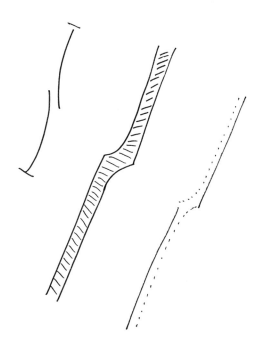

**COIMBRA FOOTBRIDGE, COIMBRA,
PORTUGAL, 2004–06
DESIGN:** CECIL BALMOND, ARUP WITH ANTÓNIO
ADÃO DA FONSECA, AFA

Photograph: On each face of the bridge the support is at the edge which leaves one half highlighted in full elevation, the other in shadow when the sun shines – the optical effect from down river is a bridge that appears not to meet!

Sketch: From each side of a river bank two arcs curve in plan and do not meet. Joining them up provides a unique solution to this footbridge, which uses the offset in plan as a dynamic experience of crossing but also finding that the shift helps with lateral stability. CB

# ÉTONNEZ-MOI
## STEFANO BOERI AND HANS ULRICH OBRIST

*Étonnez-moi*! (Surprise me!), Sergei Diaghilev once challenged Jean Cocteau in a now legendary exchange. A century later, at a time when culture is becoming increasingly globalised and the homogenisation of world architecture is a very real threat, this sense of *étonnez-moi* is crucial. There is an urgent need to generate an architecture that is receptive to interlocking spaces, that creates bridges spanning old and new, that sets up a negotiation between the local and the global. In their work, Álvaro Siza and Eduardo Souto de Moura do just this, resisting homogenising forces, retaining variety through an acknowledgement and celebration of local differences. They have achieved international acclaim for their vernacular architecture, which conserves the regional style of the places in which they build, using simple materials and linear shapes and morphologies. Siza's Portuguese Pavilion for Expo '98, Lisbon, for example, an extrordinary veil of concrete designed for the world fair, and Souto de Moura's 30,000-seat Braga football stadium for Euro 2004,

which emerges like an amphitheatre from the rock, take a 'glocal' approach, being global devices that are nevertheless locally determined.

At the heart of their relationship is great friendship, reminiscent of the alliances struck up between the avant-garde artists of the 1920s, and summed up in the words of Peter Smithson: 'Friendship is the base: affection, love in fact, and some strands of common intention.' They have known each other for more than thirty years. From 1974 to 1979, Souto de Moura worked in Siza's practice. Since then they have collaborated on several projects, including the Helsinki Museum of Contemporary Art (1992–93), and the Portuguese Pavilion for Expo '98, Lisbon, and for Expo 2000, Hanover, both with Cecil Balmond.

They have worked in numerous countries in Europe, the United States and Asia, but they are firmly based in the specific locality of Porto. They share the same office building (a four-storey riverside structure designed by Siza), which is also the headquarters of their maestro Fernando Tavora. This multi-generation office not only represents an astonishing compression of creativity, but also provides a sort of living biography, a lineage, of Portuguese cultural life. They belong to the history and geography of this location, and one cannot imagine them being located elsewhere. Thus their office is a glocal place – both global and local in its scope.

The Serpentine Gallery is also glocal: it is rooted in Kensington Gardens but wired up to the rest of the world. It is a place that is both physically stable and culturally vibrant; a permanent place that hosts and produces temporary events. In this sense, Siza and Souto de Moura constitute the perfect team to realise a building on this site.

This is also true of their collaborator, the structural engineer Cecil Balmond, who is acknowledged worldwide for his magical ability to render stable any kind of uncertain, mobile, fluid construction. The Balmond lesson is that the stability of a building can be achieved on the one hand through its lightness, which gives it the capacity to absorb tremors and vibrations, and on the other through the adaptation of existing structures into new, limber ones for the future. This looking forward sometimes means looking back. For the Serpentine Pavilion, Balmond and the architects studied historical, vernacular forms – from English farmhouses to Japanese shoes – in order to achieve solutions to working with an interlocking wooden grid.

A pavilion is an 'arche-building' – an original, archetypal structure, a simple shelter, a basic cell, which triggers thoughts about the most fundamental human needs. As such, it can be the site of many surprises. With the Serpentine Pavilion 2005, Siza, Souto de Moura and Balmond have not only accepted, but triumphantly met Diaghilev's famous challenge.

Serpentine Gallery
Pavilion 2005
Interior view drawing
© 2005 Álvaro Siza

82

# ÁLVARO SIZA AND EDUARDO SOUTO DE MOURA

## IN CONVERSATION WITH HANS ULRICH OBRIST

left:
Álvaro Siza (right) and
Eduardo Souto de Moura

right:
Serpentine Gallery
Pavilion 2005
Design evolution drawing
© 2005 Eduardo Souto de
Moura

**HANS ULRICH OBRIST:** You've collaborated on a number of projects, but you also work separately. Could you tell me about the process of working together on the Serpentine Pavilion? In the art world there's a lot of collaboration among visual artists, and in the field of philosophy, for example, people like Gilles Deleuze and Félix Guattari write books together, but I'm curious about how collaboration functions in architecture, in terms of the actual process.

**EDUARDO SOUTO DE MOURA:** I've known Siza for more than thirty years. The way we work is different, but I respect his approach and we're friends. We have dinner; we talk about ideas.

**ÁLVARO SIZA:** Eduardo and I often have opposing ideas, but that's very good. It's amusing to discuss our differences, and I sometimes tell Eduardo, 'This is Neo Plasticism'. It's a dialectical process; I'm not Eduardo's collaborator and Eduardo's not mine.

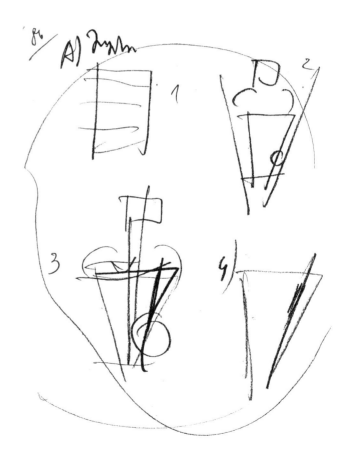

**ESM:** In terms of this project, I visited the plot first, and then we discussed the idea that it would be interesting to make, not an abstract thing, as the other architects had, but something linked with the big tree and the Gallery itself. And when Siza started drawing, our first idea was a rectangular structure that is distorted to skirt around the tree on the right. I proposed a steel structure but Siza said 'No, what about a wooden

structure, something more "poor|" like Arte Povera?' We worked next to each other at a table, endlessly swapping sketches until the concept appeared. Then when I presented it, everyone asked 'What's the concept?' Because these days the concept is like an alibi for the solution. The Pavilion is linked with the other elements – it isn't an autonomous building and it isn't meant to tell a narrative story – so the concept is 'architecture' itself.

**ÁS:** After we'd agreed to make a Pavilion that would link with the Neo-classical gallery and would explore the space between the two buildings, which is like an oval, we had our first discussions with Cecil Balmond, who met with us in Porto. And Eduardo went to London three times. We didn't have much time, so we discussed with Cecil how to build it quickly and precisely and how to solve the detailing and the way in which the wood pieces connected. And the rest we developed further via fax, telephone, e-mail and so on.

**HUO:** Did you make the drawings together or did one of you make them and then the other one edited them? Does it work like a *cadavre exquis* or like a palimpsest? How does the drawing process work with two authors?

**ÁS:** We work alone, but also together, at a table. There's a drawing, for example, that includes sketches made both by Eduardo and by me. And we make mutual comments and reciprocal criticisms of the ideas, like, 'This isn't right because …', and so on. And step by step a clear idea emerges. So it was like two pianists playing two pianos, improvising like jazz musicians.

**HUO:** Your works always take into account urban complexity, and I was wondering if you could talk a little bit about that, in relation to this London venue, where the Pavilion is situated next to a gallery in a park within the city.

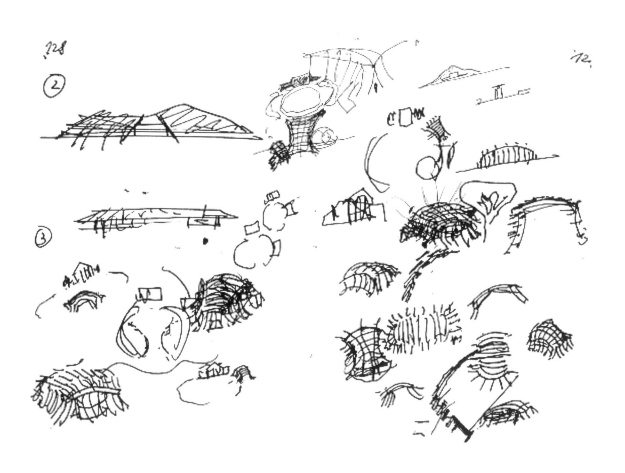

**ÁS:** There's always a relationship with the context whether we want it or not. Even buildings that at first present a sense of rupture, are in the end related to their context, and their success comes from this contrast with their setting. The Serpentine is in a park, but a street passes nearby, with cars visible. So there's the presence of the Serpentine building, as well as the tree and the pathway, and these are the things we used to find our idea. I imagine even if you worked in a desert the dunes would establish suggestions for the building, so in architecture we always use this idea of relationship.

**HUO:** Does this link to Italo Calvino's notion of the 'invisible city' – to the idea of somehow making the invisible city visible?

**ÁS:** Yes. The way we look at and discover the city in which we're working is one of the most important tools for the project. If I'm working in London or in Berlin, I'll have two very different

suggestions. And these provide the impulse for developing an idea. The atmosphere is the most important element – more important than the programme, or the budget – when developing a proposal.

**HUO:** I also wanted to ask you about interior complexity, because I think the whole idea of the pavilion is very interesting in the sense that it's not only about a facade, but about the interior.

**ESM:** We had the idea of making the Pavilion open because it's a summer building. So the bottom one metre thirty of the structure is absolutely open. This means that people who are seated can look directly into the open, but when they stand up the translucent plastic cladding gives the sensation of being inside, although it's very open and transparent. So the first sketches, which were conducted in relation to some sculptures and paintings, some organic forms, gradually became more complex. To give you an idea, the porticoes were originally more or less the same on the four sides of the building – slightly curved – but as we developed the project, we gradually straightened them out, so that those in front of the Serpentine building, for instance, became absolutely vertical. So, added to the curve of the oval that defines the building, there's a movement from the porticoes in the periphery to those in the centre. The junction of the two curved pillars formed a sort of fissure at each corner, and then we decided to put a kind of entrance at two of these points. One is a wooden structure that juts out and gives a view concentrated on the Serpentine building, the other leads to the pathway. And then we had the idea to incorporate ventilation chimneys in the

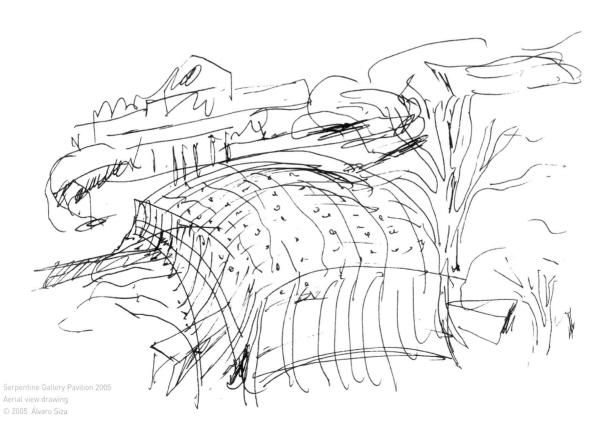

Serpentine Gallery Pavilion 2005
Aerial view drawing
© 2005 Álvaro Siza

Serpentine Gallery Pavilion 2005
Interior view drawing
© 2005 Eduardo Souto de Moura

roof and around the building, and to install solar lamps that convert the energy of the sun into illumination in the evening.

**HUO:** Could you talk a little bit about your choice of materials?

**ESM:** We decided not to make a high-tech building because we wanted something like Arte Povera. We wanted something natural. And we started to study, with Cecil, old buildings made of wood, such as some farms in England, looking at the way the pieces of wood are joined. We also looked at Japanese architecture, studying the natural detailing. The initial idea was to make the building flat and the same height as the Serpentine building, but the topography of the site slopes a little towards the road and Cecil proposed that we deform the grid on the roof and on the elevation near the tree. This means that the other elevation, on the Serpentine building side, starts in the corner at

an angle and becomes vertical in the middle, so we have a tension between the two buildings. And we made this distortion, not for aesthetic reasons, but because of the conditions of the site, and these angles, deformations, variations in height, create the correct building form. Similarly, the way in which we put the pieces of wood together, and the complexity of each one is not something voluntary but the way to resolve a problem.

**ÁS:** The deformation in front of the Serpentine building gives a suggestion of the orientation of the Pavilion, creating a facade on one side. So the idea of the Pavilion could be the same in every site, but the process of building in a way obliged us to make that distortion, which detaches that side of the building from the others.

**HUO:** That leads me also to another question: the notion of exhibition. The pavilion is linked in two ways to the world of exhibition: on the one hand, obviously, through this architectural form's history as a medium of world fairs, and secondly through its juxtaposition to the Serpentine Gallery, which is a venue for art exhibitions. Also, a pavilion sets up a kind of laboratory condition where new ideas can be tested that would be more difficult to explore in a larger building. Its temporary nature allows a higher degree of experimentation. Could you talk about your relationship to the world of exhibitions?

**ÁS:** I've made a number of museums, including the Serralves Museum of Contemporary Art in Porto, as well as being involved in the exhibition there, *Álvaro Siza On Display – Museums and Exhibition Spaces*, and Eduardo has made two museums, Grão Vasco Museum in an old convent in Portugal and the Portuguese Photographic Centre in a former prison and courts building. But the Serpentine Pavilion is very different. It's a temporary building, very open, very free, where the activities are not clearly defined. It's like a meeting point. There will be events there and a conference, and so on, but it's quite different from museums, and from the other exhibition spaces I've experimented with. For instance, one doesn't have to worry about the infrastructure, which elsewhere would be so important; here it's much more free because it's temporary. We also designed the furniture, which has a very close connection to the rest of the building in terms of the materials and the form and so on. So I don't think there is much of a relationship between this and the other exhibition spaces we've done, except that it's a varied-activity building and is next to an art gallery. But the relationship to art in general is very strong. Eduardo has already spoken of the influence of Arte Povera, and during the development of the drawing we quickly discovered a relationship with paintings and sculpture, such as the paintings of the famous Portuguese artist Maria Elena Vieira da Silva, and the sculpture of Louise Bourgeois. We discovered some affinities with this kind of work and the reason for this is that we were free from the conditions of function, infrastructure and so on.

**HUO:** In terms of the organic materials, in previous interviews you've talked about the building as a 'living creator'. Could you talk a bit about this?

**ESM:** As so often happens with architecture, organic, even animal forms can help to develop a project. And throughout the centuries, architecture has made figurative reference to organic forms. The buildings of Palladio, for example, are full of faces, eyes and noses and other bodily organs. I'm not referring to the invention of final forms, but rather to the help that the architecture receives from natural and organic shapes. And in a way the development of the project sets it free from these suggestions, which can become too demonstrative. So it's not the final objective, but it helps, to establish these relations. You'll see,

for instance, that the curve of the roof has some resemblance to the back of an animal – a pig or an elephant. But this merely helps one to grow imaginatively beyond the problems that exist – the discipline of the structure, the conditions of building quickly and cheaply, and so on.

**ÁS:** When we talk about organic or animal forms, we don't mean that we're making a direct analogy. What's important is the attitude, the shape and structure, the feeling of calm, for example, as if the animal were sleeping. When you design, you need some reference, because initially you have nothing. And you use this as a starting point, but it's the means to an end and not the final goal. You want to make it a bit like an elephant, and thinking about the attitude of an elephant can give you something to help you arrive at the final shape. With the pillars, for instance, where they make contact with the ground, we were thinking about legs, and about

Japanese shoes, but only the way in which a Japanese shoe touches the floor. We were also referencing some vernacular English architecture – the old farms that Cecil showed us – and the way in which a lot of these wood structures link with and touch the land.

**HUO:** Do the two of you have any unrealised collaborative projects that you'd like to see built?

**ÁS:** I would single out a plan we developed for Macau, China (1983-84), which was built, but not according to the proposed scheme, and the competition for the Helsinki Contemporary Art Museum of 1992.

**ESM:** It's natural that some projects don't get built, because architecture is a social art. If a painter decides to make a painting he can make whatever painting he likes. But we need a lot of money and a team to build the project and we have to deal with the political conditions, so we can't just decide to build or not to build. But we can use the project like a laboratory, to check forms, details etc that can be used again in the next project.

**ÁS:** Every architect has many projects in which he was deeply engaged but that in the end, for one reason or another, didn't work out. You lose competitions and so on. But they don't disappear. The research done for each project passes on to the others – not directly as a form, or as an image, but as an experience in developing the many possibilities that exist in architecture.

# CECIL BALMOND

## IN CONVERSATION WITH STEFANO BOERI AND HANS ULRICH OBRIST

**STEFANO BOERI:** Cecil, when I think of you, I immediately think: 'Well, here we have the "mission impossible" engineer.' But in the case of the Serpentine, you're no longer working to make an impossible architecture stable, but to make a temporary shelter vibrant. So the first question I wanted to ask you is about this idea of the shelter as a structure, an autonomous skin. Could tell me a little bit about the Serpentine project as a structure?

**CECIL BALMOND:** I'm glad you use that word 'structure' because the notion of structure as architecture, in a classical sense, is what the Serpentine Pavilion is about: form, structure, architecture. But for me these projects are also attempts to explore a new aesthetic using structure as a forensic, so that in each of the pavilions there have been specific interventions that shift the eye and produce a certain kind of dynamic perspective in new configurations. The idea of shelter as a passive structure is overtaken by an active component that you enter. These pavilions in particular have an animate sense of geometry; they give a sense of movement when you're in them. It's the opposite of shelter as a protection; it's a catalyst. You engage with the form, and it does things – it shifts and moves.

**HANS ULRICH OBRIST:** So in a sense it's not passive, it's a trigger?

**CB:** It's hard to put your finger on, of course, what the aesthetic sense does, but in the pavilions I've worked on, your eye moves outwards in a way that projects you out of the pavilion. It's not shelter in the traditional sense of 'cave', but something you engage with – as you say, a trigger that fires you out of your senses in some way.

**HUO:** When I spoke with Álvaro and Eduardo I asked them about their very unusual

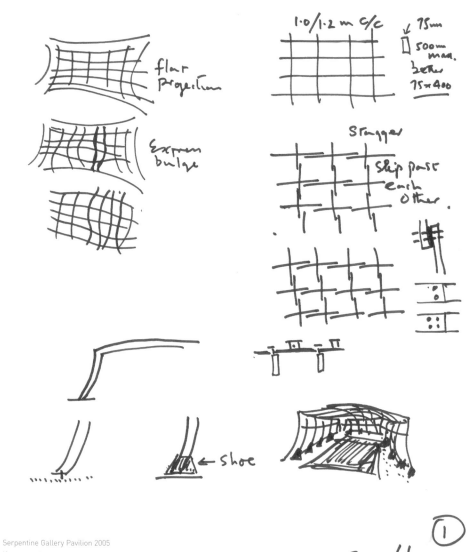

flat Projection

Expand bulge

1.0/1.2 m c/c

↓ 75mm
□ 500mm max.
3 other
75×400

Stagger

Skip pass each other.

← shoe

CB 27/1/05

①

collaboration. Álvaro said that he's not Eduardo's collaborator, and nor is Eduardo his collaborator. It's more like a dialectical process. Can you tell me about this whole notion of the way you collaborate with architects in general, and then if the Serpentine Pavilion was different – in other words, if working with two other people is different from just one?

**CB:** My typical collaborations with Rem Koolhaas, Toyo Ito, Daniel Libeskind etc. have two components: a dialectic component and a collaborative component. I try to pose the questions as much as providing answers and in that sense I think my work is trying to extend the architectural hypothesis, whatever that is, whether it's for a library or a pavilion. I worked with Siza on the Portuguese Pavilion for Expo '98, Lisbon, that lovely sailing curve in space, and then I also worked with Siza and Eduardo on the Portuguese Pavilion for Expo 2000, Hanover. And Siza is correct: it isn't a collaboration.

Eduardo doesn't work for Siza, but Siza has been a guru, if you like, to Eduardo. And Eduardo has grown his own identity. When we worked on the Hanover pavilion, Siza tackled the overall form and I developed the roof in particular with Siza and Eduardo, but Eduardo developed all the material aspects and textures. It's a dialogue between Siza and Eduardo. If Eduardo is driving the design, then Siza will collaborate in a different way. This year there was a three-part dialogue going on, with us coming to conclusions quite easily because of the long-term collaboration and understanding that Eduardo has with Siza and the understanding I've grown with Siza in the past. I worked with Siza on two built projects and on a major project that we never realized in Sicily.

**HUO:** So you have an unrealized project together, you and Siza?

**CB:** Yes, a marvellous one. It was for the football games. Maybe it was to do with the cycling

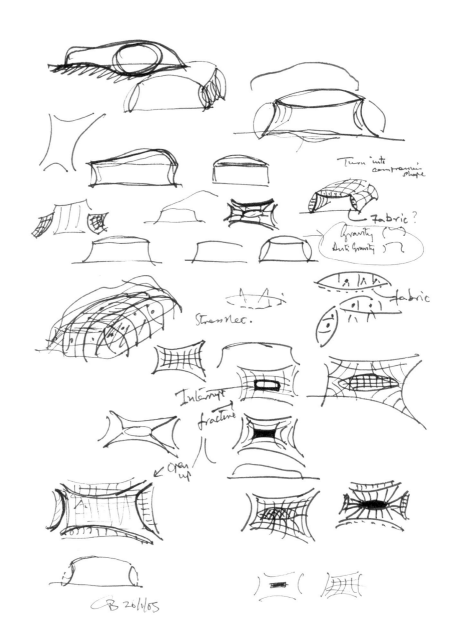

championships as well – well some sporting event anyway, about six years ago, and as always in Sicily the problem was with the site. Siza and I had already worked on the Portuguese Pavilion at Expo, which was very successful. He then invited me to work with him on this Palermo project. It wasn't a competition. And it was great. It was a stadium, not quite Olympic size but reflecting the classical Greek sort of horseshoe stadium. There were four or five other buildings. The stadium design was interesting: we did it with stone, using new forms and techniques.

I grew to know Siza and found him a very interesting man to work with. I enjoyed our evenings together. Eduardo, I got to know subsequently, and visited his office. It was interesting how the collaborations grew. I introduced my Portuguese partners António Adão da Fonseca to Siza, and a guy called Rui Furtado to Eduardo, who's done a lot of work now with him. So it's a nice sort of feeling of community.

**HUO:** I made some interviews with Peter Smithson in 2000, and we spoke about this whole idea that pavilions can be very important laboratories for architecture. They're non-permanent solutions that can be tested and can go further than other structures. I was wondering how you see this, if you would agree with Smithson?

**CB:** I do. I use these forms to provide an aesthetic of structure. So if you take the very first one I did, with Libeskind, it was a wrapping in space; we wanted to imitate the Victoria & Albert Museum spiral form slightly. But having said that, if you looked at those panels, the way they were framed, they weren't conventional. I used rapid movement lines as bracing, zigzagging in space on each plane, adding momentum to the effect of leaning and wrapping. It was pushing the boundaries of how to do bracing and how to see its patterns accelerating the oblique. With Ito we discussed algorithm. And there was a little repeated rule at work, a sort of abstract engine, that went to create the whole pattern, and realised that amazing pavilion with all its cross lines. It was one of the most photographed pavilions I can remember. Many people came up to me and said, 'We know something's going on, but we don't know what.' There was this underlying rigour that was felt, some kind of an order behind what looked like randomness, which is very much what I've been experimenting with for years. On this pavilion, if you look at the sketch drawing and then look at the permanent thing, it's almost identical. It's a good example of a simple, abstract idea being developed into a new kind of aesthetic where a box form, through its surface patterns, completely deprives the box of a sense of enclosure. Every corner moves differently. If you're in there it's like a time capsule; your eye just moves round the criss- crosses and then you move out. And the corners also, because they're configured so differently, have no

classification. It's a box form that implies a right angle and yet has none that are sharply defined. The pavilion structures are like little villas, classic laboratories of architecture. And this one we're doing now with Siza and Eduardo began with a simple grid shell. In the spirit of what you just said about the project being a laboratory, we improvised a 'shuffling' grid. Siza said, 'Lets go for a strong, primitive kind of vernacular architectural feel', and he mentioned Arte Povera. It strictly isn't, but we used timber. And I proposed an offset grid using old-fashioned mortice and tenon joints.

**HUO:** He mentioned Arte Povera in our interview.

**CB:** It's not strictly Arte Povera because we're using high-tech polycarbonates for the skin and complex manufacturing techniques. If you look at the first sketch Siza proposed, it was a grid shell. If we just took it as a form and replied to that, it would have been just another grid shell. Instead, an offset grid proposed a shifting sense of rhythm, so you don't get the monotonous, regular lattice rhythm. Here, the form moves. And again, I predict your eye will start following the lines, just as in the pavilion with Ito. You start following the structure, and something else happens. You don't read the structure. We used old techniques of medieval architecture in a mortice and tenon joint to assemble the form with the minimum of connection. But we used a high-tech software programme to cut and form the angled members. The polycarbonate panels house a chimney in which a solar light is used. The skin is like an upholstery. Siza wanted a kind of 'spotted' feeling to the form.

**SB:** The laboratory notion leads to the question of Buckminster Fuller. On the one hand everybody speaks about him and at the same time there's a sort of amnesia where he's concerned, so I thought it would be interesting if you could talk about Buckminster Fuller.

**CB:** Buckminster Fuller? I agree everyone talks about him because there's a certain boldness and also, frankly, a good salesmanship on his own part. But he had a lasting contribution to make in the sense of the Geodesic Dome, taking out the spherical surface with a certain nodal pattern. Buckminster Fuller is talked about a lot because of those contributions, but there is also, I agree with you, amnesia. In truth, if I'm speaking personally, though I respect the work, I haven't been inspired by it. Fuller came in with an essential classical notion of space that was formed in a closed manner, evenly distributed, and centred, whereas what I'm looking at has been more to do with local ideas of adjacency and connection. He was interested in global frameworks and I'm more interested in the local individual actions that lead to a variable complexity, more in the way of serial patterns, and you see that interest as a very visible rhythm moving round the Serpentine form this year as well.

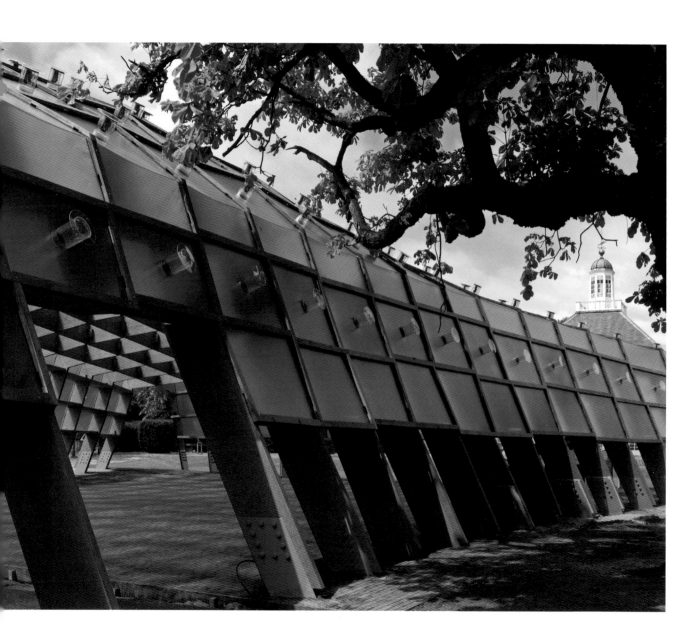

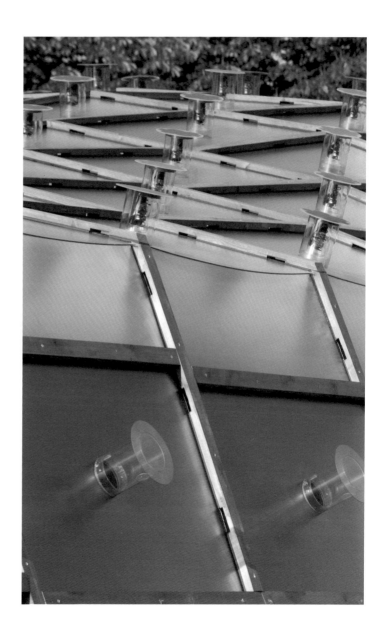

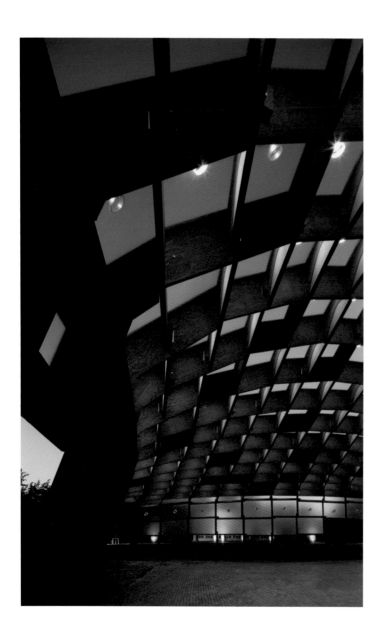

# TECHNICAL DRAWINGS

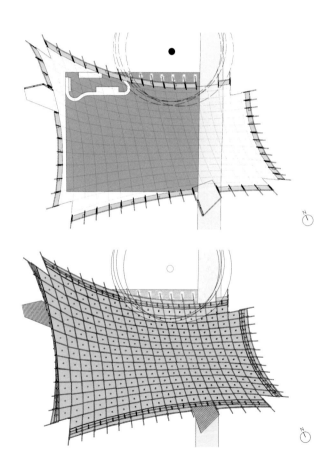

left: Serpentine Gallery
Pavilion 2005
Ground plan and roof plan

right: Serpentine Gallery
Pavilion 2005
Site plan

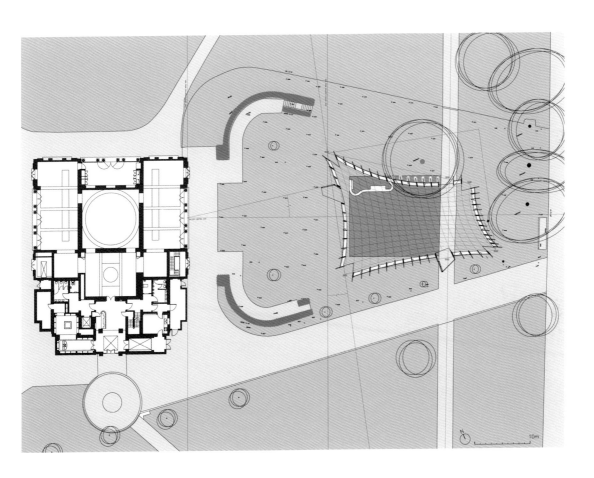

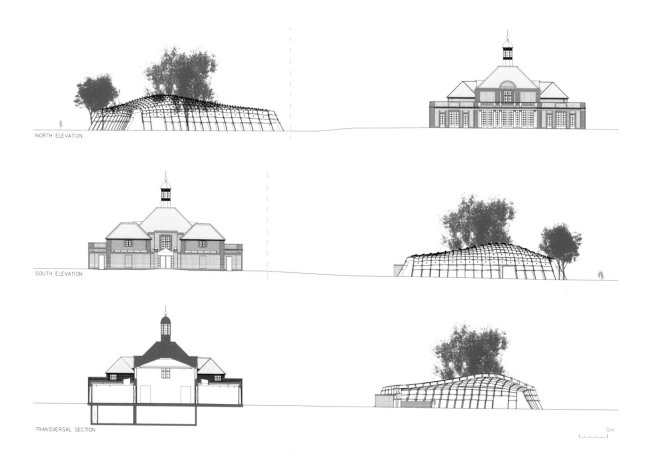

NORTH ELEVATION

SOUTH ELEVATION

TRANSVERSAL SECTION

5m

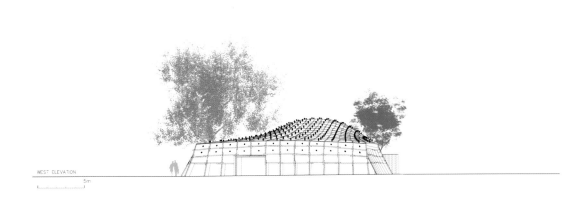

WEST ELEVATION

5m

EAST ELEVATION

5m

# TECHNICAL DESCRIPTION

**The Pavilion is a column-free enclosure approximately 25 m x 15 m in plan. The walls are typically 3 m tall and the roof reaches a maximum height of 5.5 m above ground.**

At 400 m², the Pavilion is larger than in previous years. It synthesises contemporary design and fabrication techniques with a traditional construction vernacular. The column-free roof and walls are formed from an undulating, offset grid of timber beams. The geometry is based on a quadrilateral plan and has wall and roof curvatures defined by arcs in plan and elevation respectively.

The structural pattern was developed from the architects' initial grid, creating an offset aesthetic, in order to animate the structure. It is built up from 427 unique timber beams that are linked in a shifting rhythm, far removed from the static nature of normal grillage structures, to create the dramatic 17 m clear span. The grillage has a typical grid-unit dimension of between 1 and 1.5 m.

The structure, in which interlocking elements are arranged in a mutually supporting pattern, allows each individual element to have simple mortice-and-tenon connections, yet is able to maintain the overall bending stiffness. It was created as an evolution of the 'lamella' barrel-vault roofs developed in Germany in the early 1920s. While traditional lamellas were built from identical elements, however, each element of the Pavilion is unique, having a different length and inclination. This geometric freedom enables the precise expression of the complex form demanded by the architects. The reciprocal beam system creates a continuous structure that runs from the roof down to form the walls of the Pavilion.

Kerto-LVL Grade Q, laminated veneers of Finnish Spruce with typical depth 550 mm and width 69 mm, were used for high strength and dimensional stability. The individual geometries of the 427 elements (each with thirty-six points that had to be exactly defined using X,Y and Z co-ordinates) were generated digitally and mapped out using a project-specific script. The 3D output enabled direct communication between the design team and the timber fabricators. All the timber elements were prefabricated using 5-axes CNC machining technology.

The interlocking beams also demanded that a unique erection sequence be defined; the construction started at one corner and radiated out to finish at the opposite extreme.

The Pavilion is clad externally with 248 translucent, 5 mm thick polycarbonate panels (also cut using CNC machining) that each incorporate an autonomous solar-powered light.

Hamish Nevile, Arup

# DESIGN TEAM

**Architectural Design**
Álvaro Siza
Eduardo Souto de Moura
Cecil Balmond
Tiago Figueiredo
Tiago Coelho
Atsushi Ueno

**Integrated Design:** Arup
Hamish Nevile
Martin Self
Lip Chiong
Charles Walker
Steve Walker
Andrew Hall
Anthony Ferguson
Andrew Lawrence

**Porto Architectural/**
**Structural Liaison:** AFA
António Adão da Fonseca
Rui Furtado
Raul Serafim

**Project Advisors**
Peter Rogers, Stanhope plc
Lord Palumbo, Chairman,
Serpentine Gallery
Zaha Hadid, Trustee,
Serpentine Gallery

**Project Director**
Julia Peyton-Jones, Serpentine Gallery

**Project Manager**
Mark Robinson

**Project Organizer**
Rebecca Morrill, Serpentine Gallery

**Planning and Building Control**
City of Westminster Planning and
Transportation Department

**Cost Consultant**
Davis Langdon

**Town Planning**
DP9

**Planning Supervisor**
Bovis Lend Lease

**Landscaping Consultant**
Arabella Lennox-Boyd

**Sale of the Pavilion**
Knight Frank

**Construction Management**
Bovis Lend Lease

**Contractors**
John Doyle Group
(Ground works and welfare)
Screwfast Ltd (Ground anchors)
GTL Partnership Ltd
William Hare (Structural steel)
Laing O'Rourke (Site equipment)
Finnforest Merk
(Structural timber frame and covering)
Bay Plastics
DB Construct
Fixers Ltd
Peri Ltd
Sikken
Solar Century (lighting)
Bowles & Wyer
(Landscaping and blockwork)
Irvine Whitlock
Penton Group (Bar construction)
T Clarke (Small power)
S. Design (Furniture)
Keltbray (Dismantling)
SES Ltd (Surveying)

**Security**
Clipfine

# ÁLVARO SIZA
## SELECTED BIOGRAPHY

**PROJECTS ARE LISTED UNDER THE YEAR OF THEIR FIRST CONCEPT PHASE; THE YEAR OF COMPLETION, IF DIFFERENT, IS NOTED IN PARENTHESIS.**

**1933**
Born Matosinhos, near Porto, Portugal

**1949–55**
Studied at the School of Architecture, University of Porto

**1954**
Four Houses, Matosinhos, Porto, Portugal (1957)

**1955–58**
Worked with the architect Fernando Távora

**1958**
Tea House, Boa Nova, Leça da Palmeira, Porto, Portugal, with Alberto Neves, António Meneres, Botelho Dias and Joaquim Sampaio) (1963)
Quinta da Conceição Swimming Pool, Matosinhos, Porto, Portugal (1965)

**1961**
Ocean Swimming Pool, Leça da Palmeira, Porto, Portugal (1966)

**1962**
Ferreira da Costa House, Matosinhos, Porto, Portugal (1965)

**1964**
Alves Costa House, Moledo do Monho, Portugal (1968)

**1966–69**
Taught at School of Architecture, University of Porto

**1967**
Manuel Magalhães House, Combatentes Avenue, Porto, Portugal (1970)

**1969**
Project for office block, Avenida da Ponte, Porto, Portugal

**1970**
Housing Project, Caxinas, Vila do Conde, Portugal (1972) (partly constructed, later modified)

**1971**
Alcino Cardoso House, Moledxo do Minho, Portugal (1973)
Pinto and Sotto Mayor Bank, Oliveira de Azeméis, Portugal (1974)

**1972**
Pinto and Sotto Mayor Bank, Lamego, Portugal (1973)

**1973**
Carlos Beires House, Póvoa de Varzim, Portugal (1976)

**1974**
SAAL residental complex, São Victor, Porto, Portugal (1977)

**1975**
SAAL Social Housing, Bouça, Porto, Portugal (1st phase completed 1977, 2nd phase, 2005)

**1976**
Appointed Professor of Construction, School of Architecture, University of Porto, Portugal
António Carlos Siza House, Santo Tirso, Porto, Portugal (1978)

**1977**
Quinta da Malagueira Social Housing, Évora, Portugal (1995)

**1980**
Apartment building, Schlesisches Tor, Kreuzberg, West Berlin, with Peter Brinkert (1984)
Avelino Duarte House, Ovar, Portugal (1984)

**1982**
Borges and Irmão Bank, Vila do Conde, Portugal (1986)

**1983**
Schilderswijk Social Housing Project, The Hague, Netherlands (1988)

**1984**
David Vieira de Castro House, Famalicão, Portugal (1999)
Luís Figueiredo House, Gondomar, Porto, Portugal (1994)
Kindergarten 'João de Deus', Penafiel, Portugal (1991)
Two houses and shops, Schilderswijk-Centrum, The Hague, Netherlands (1988)

**1985**
Van der Vannepark Garden, Schilderswijk-West, The Hague, Netherlands (1988)
Quinta da Póvoa, Faculty of Architecture, Porto, Portugal (1986)
Carlos Ramos Pavilion, Faculty of Architecture, Porto, Portugal (1986)

**1986**
Teacher Training College, Setúbal, Portugal (1993)

**1987**
Faculty of Architecture, Porto, Portugal (1994)

**1988**
Water Tower (1989) and Library (1995), Aveiro University, Portugal (1989)

Galician Centre for Contemporary Art,
  Santiago de Compostela, Spain (1993)
**1989**
Ferreira de Castro Office Building, Oliveira
  de Azeméis, Portugal (1995)
Quinto de Santo, Ovidio, Portugal 1989–92/
  1997–2001)
**1990**
Santa Maria Church and Parochial Centre,
  Marco de Canavezes, Portugal (1996)
Meteorological Centre for Olympic Village
  and MOPU Headquarters, Barcelona,
  Spain (1992)
Project for Valencia University Rectory and
  Law Library, Valencia, Spain
**1991**
Museum of Contemporary Art, Serralves
  Foundation, Porto, Portugal (1999)
Boavista Tourism Complex, Porto, Portugal
  (with António Madurcira) (1998)
Reconstruction of the Chiado area,
  Lisbon (1994)
Vitra International, Furniture Factory
  Building, Weil-am-Rhein, Germany (1994)
**1992**
Baixa/Chiado Underground Station, Lisbon,
  Portugal (1998)
Project for Helsinki Museum of
  Contemporary Art, Finland, with Eduardo
  Souto de Moura
Terraços de Bragança, Lisbon,
  Portugal (2004)
**1993**
Revigrés showroom, Agueda,

Portugal (1997)
Architect's Office, Aleixo, Porto,
  Portugal (1997)
Faculty of Media Sciences, Santiago
  de Compostela, Spain (2000)
**1995**
Portuguese Pavilion for Expo '98, Lisbon,
  Portugal (1998)
Rectory of Alicante University, Spain (1997)
APDL – Harbour of Leixões Administrative
  Building, Matosinhos, Porto, Portugal
  (2001)
Van Middelem-Dupont House, Oudenburg,
  Belgium (2001)
Project for Stedelijk Museum (extension),
  Pauluspotterstraat, Amsterdam,
  Netherlands
**1996**
Project for pier, Thessaloniki, Greece
**1997**
Project for Manzana del Revellín Cultural
  Centre, Ceuta, Spain
Rosario Municipal Centre, Rosario,
  Argentina (2004)
**1998**
Villa Colonnese, Vicenza, Italy (under
  construction)
Iberê Camargo Foundation, Avenida Padre
  Cacique, Porto Alegre, Brazil (under
  construction)
**1999**
Portuguese Pavilion Expo 2000, Hanover,
  with Eduardo Souto de Moura (2000)
  (reconstructed in Coimbra, 2003)

**2002**
Project for Gist-Brocades Apartment
  Building, Matosinhos, Porto, Portugal,
  with Eduardo Souto de Moura
Renovation of Rotunda da Boavista,
  with Eduardo Souto de Moura (2004)
**2003**
Municipio Linea 1 & 6 station and public
  square, Naples, Italy, with Eduardo Souto
  de Moura (in progress)
Boavista overground metro line, Porto,
  Portugal, with Eduardo Souto de Moura
  (in progress)
**2005**
Renovation of Aliados Avenue, Porto,
  Portugal with Eduardo Souto de Moura
  (in progress)

**AWARDS**
**1982**
Prize for Architecture from The Portuguese
  Department of the International
  Association of Art Critics
**1987**
Award from the Portuguese Architects
  Association
**1988**
Gold Medal from the Colegio de
  Architectos, Spain
Gold Medal from the Alvar Aalto
  Foundation
Prince of Wales Prize in Urban Design
  from Harvard University, Massachusetts
European Architecture Award from the

Economic European Comunity/Mies van
der Rohe Foundation, Barcelona
**1992**
Pritzker Prize from the Hyatt Foundation
of Chicago
**1993**
National Prize of Architecture from the
Portuguese Architects Association
**1994**
Dr H.P. Berlagestichting Prize
Gubbio Prize/Associazione Nazionale
Centri Storico-Artistici
**1995**
Gold Medal, Nara World Architecture
Exposition
International Award Architetture di Pietra,
Fiera di Verona
**1996**
Secil Prize for Architecture
**1997**
Manuel de la Dehesa Award from
Menendez Pelayo University,
Santander
**1998**
Arnold W. Brunner Memorial Prize from
the American Academy of Arts and
Letters, New York
The Premio IberFAD de Arquitectura from
Foment de les Arts Decoratives,
Barcelona
Praemium Imperiale from the Japan Art
Association, Tokyo

Gold Medal from the Circulo de Bellas
Artes, Madrid
**1999**
Grã-Cruz da Ordem do Infante D. Henrique
from the Presidency of the Portuguese
Republic and the Leca Prize of
Construction '98
**2000**
Premio Internazionale di Architettura
Sacra from the Fondazione Frate
Sole, Pavia
Secil Prize for Architecture
**2001**
Wolf Prize for the Arts (Architecture) from
the Wolf Foundation, Israel
Alexandre Herculano National Architecture
Prize, Lisbon
**2002**
International Compostela Prizel, Xunta da
Galicia, Santiago de Compostela
International Medal for the Arts from
Consejera de las Artes, Madrid
Golden Lion, 8th International Architecture
Exhibition, Venice Biennale, Italy
Best Professional Trajectory in
Architecture, III Biennale Ibero-American
in Architecture and Civil Engineering,
Santiago
Personality of the Year 2002 from Foreign
Press Association
Best International Trajectory in
Architecture – Vitruvio 2002 from the

National Belas Artes Museum,
Buenos Aires
**2003**
Medal of Touristic Merit, Inland Revenue
Department, Lisbon
Palladio d'Oro, Vicenza Town Hall
Special Mark of Honour, Castilla La
Mancha Oficial College of Architects,
Guadalajara

**HONORARY DOCTORATES**
**1992**
University of Valencia
**1993**
École Polithécnique Federal
de Lausanne
**1995**
Palermo University
Menendez Pelayo University, Santander
Universidad Nacional de Ingeniería
de Lima
**1997**
University of Coimbra
**1999**
Universidade Lusíada
**2000**
University of Paraíba, João Pessoa

# ÁLVARO SIZA
# SELECTED BIBLIOGRAPHY

## 1986
*Álvaro Siza: Poetic Profession.* Kenneth Frampton, Nuno Portas, Alexandre Alves Costa. Milan: Electa/London: The Architectural Press

## 1990
*Álvaro Siza Architectures 1980–1990.* Alexandre Alves Costa. Paris: Centre Georges Pompidou

## 1992
*Álvaro Siza.* Brigitte Fleck. Basel, Boston, Berlin: Birkhauser Verlag AG

## 1993
*Álvaro Siza: Works and Projects 1954–1992.* Jose Paulo Dos Santos, ed. Barcelona: Editorial Gustavo Gili SA

## 1994
*Álvaro Siza: City Sketches.* Foreword by Norman Foster, Brigitte Fleck, Wilfried Wang, Introduction by Álvaro Siza. Basel: Birkhauser Verlag AG

## 1995
*Álvaro Siza.* Brigitte Fleck. London: E & FN Spon Press
*Álvaro Siza: Works and Projects.* Pedro De Llano and Carlos Castanheira, eds. Madrid: Electa
*Álvaro Siza, 1986–1995.* Luiz Trigueiros, ed. Lisbon: Editorial Blau

## 1996
*Álvaro Siza.* Peter Testa. Basel, Boston, Berlin: Birkhauser Verlag AG

## 1997
*Álvaro Siza: Writings on Architecture.* Álvaro Siza, Antonio Angelillo, ed. Milan: Skira
*Álvaro Siza. 1954–1976.* Luiz Trigueiros, ed. Foreword by Kenneth Frampton. Introduction by Alexandre Alves Costa. Lisbon: Editorial Blau
*Álvaro Siza: The Strategy of Memory, Chiado, Lisbon.* Bernard Colenbrander. Rotterdam: Netherlands Architecture Institute

## 1998
*Álvaro Siza.* Yukio Futagawa, ed. GA Document Extra. Tokyo: ADA Edita

## 2000
*Álvaro Siza: The Complete Works.* Kenneth Frampton. London: Phaidon Press
*Álvaro Siza 1958–2000.* Richard C. Levene and Fernando Marquez Cecilia. Madrid: El Croquis, No.68/69+95 (revised)

## 2001
*Álvaro Siza: Serralves Museum.* Texts by Paulo Martins Barata, Raquel Henriques de Silva and Bernado Pinto de Almeida. Lisbon: White and Blue
*Las Ciudades de Álvaro Siza.* Carlos Castanheira and Chiaro Porcu, eds. Texts by Álvaro Siza and Nuno Higino. Madrid: Talis Comunicación International

## 2002
*Álvaro Siza.* Photography by Duccio Malagamba. London: teNeues Publishing UK Ltd

## 2003
*Álvaro Siza.* Philip Jodidio. Cologne: Taschen

## 2005
*Álvaro Siza: Private Houses.* Enrico Molteni, Alessandra Cianchetta. Milan: Skira
*Álvaro Siza: On Display.* Texts by Rudi Fuchs and Peter Testa, interview by Carlos Castanheira and João Fernandes. Porto: Museu Serralves

# EDUARDO SOUTO DE MOURA
## SELECTED BIOGRAPHY

**PROJECTS ARE LISTED UNDER THE YEAR OF THEIR FIRST CONCEPT PHASE; THE YEAR OF COMPLETION, IF DIFFERENT, IS NOTED IN PARENTHESIS.**

**1952**
Born Porto, Portugal
**1974–1979**
Worked with the architect Álvaro Siza
**1980**
Graduated from the School of
 Architecture, University of Porto
Set up own practice
Municipal Market, Braga, Portugal (1984)
**1981–1991**
Assistant Professor, Faculty of
 Architecture of Porto, Portugal
**1981**
Casa das Artes, Cultural Centre, S.E.C.,
 Porto (1991)
**1982**
House 1, Nevogilde, Porto, Portugal (1985)
House 2, Nevogilde, Porto, Portugal (1988)
**1984**
House, Quinta do Lago, Almansil,
 Algarve, Portugal (1989)
**1985**
Project for Dell'Accademia Bridge, 3rd
 International Architecture Exhibition,
 Venice Biennale, Italy
**1986**
Vilarinha Annexes, Porto, Portugal (1988)
**1987**
House, Alcanena, Torres Novas,
 Portugal (1992)
Project for Salzburg Hotel, Austria
Urban master plan for Porta dei Colli,

Palermo, Triennale of Milan, Italy
House 1, Miramar, Vila Nova de Gaia,
 Portugal (1991)
House, Av. Boavista, Porto,
 Portugal (1994)
**1988**
Urban master plan and civic buildings for
 Mondello, Palermo, Italy
**1989**
Conversion of monastery into Pousada
 Santa Maria do Bouro, Amares,
 Portugal (1997)
House, Bom Jesus, Braga, Portugal (1994)
**1990**
Department of Geosciences, Aveiro
 University, Aveiro, Portugal (1994)
House, Maia, Porto, Portugal (1993)
House, Baião, Porto, Portugal (1993)
**1991**
House, Tavira, Algarve, Portugal (1995)
Burgo Project, Boavista Avenue, Porto,
 Portugal (under construction)
House, Travessa do Souto, Moledo do
 Minho, Caminha, Portugal (1998)
**1992**
Building in Rua do Teatro, Porto,
 Portugal (1995)
Project for Helsinki Museum of
 Contemporary Art, Finland, with
 Álvaro Siza
Children's Library and Auditorium,
 Porto, Portugal (2000)

**1993**
Renovation, Grão Vasco Museum, Viseu,
 Portugal (2004)
Courtyard Houses, Matosinhos, Porto,
 Portugal (1999)
**1994**
House, Serra da Arrábida,
 Portugal (2002)
House, Cascais, Portugal (2002)
Residential Building, Liége Square,
 Porto, Portugal (2001)
**1995**
Urban master plan for Maia City, Maia
 (partially completed 2004)
Conversion for the waterfront of
 Matosinhos, Porto, Portugal,
 1st Phase (2002)
Interior exhibition space, Portuguese
 Pavilion for Expo'98, Lisbon,
 Portugal (1998)
**1997**
Interior, Armazéns do Chiado, Lisbon,
 Portugal (1999)
Conversion of prison and court building
 into Portuguese Photographic Centre,
 Porto, Portugal (2001)
Metro Stations, Porto, Portugal (2005)
Residential Building, Maia, Porto,
 Portugal (2001)
Conversion of Municipal Market into
 cultural centre, Braga, Portugal (2001)

**1998**

Silo cultural centre, NorteShopping, Matosinhos, Porto, Portugal (1999)

Cinema House for Manoel de Oliveira, Porto, Portugal (2003)

**1999**

Portuguese Pavilion for Expo 2000, Hanover, Germany, with Álvaro Siza (2000)

**2000**

Braga Stadium, Braga, Portugal (2003)

**2001**

Two houses, Fomelos, Ponte de Lima, Portugal

**2002**

Gist-Brocades Apartment Building, Matosinhos, Porto, Portugal, with Álvaro Siza (project)

Courtyard Houses, Boavista Avenue, Porto, Portugal (2005)

Renovation of historic area of Valença, Valença do Minho, Portugal (under construction)

House, Quinta da Borralha, Braga, Portugal (under construction)

Renovation of Rotunda da Boavista, with Álvaro Siza (2004)

**2003**

Centre for Contemporary Art, Bragança, Portgual (under construction)

House, Girona, Barcelona, Spain (under construction)

Project for Metro do Porto Headquarters, Porto, Portugal

Municipio Linea 1 & 6 station and public square, Naples, Italy, with Álvaro Siza (under construction)

Boavista overground metro line, Porto, Portugal, with Álvaro Siza (under construction)

**2004**

Houses, Óbidos, Portugal (under construction)

Tea house in Rotunda da Boavista, Porto, Portugal, with Álvaro Siza (in planning)

Office, hotel and residential buildings, Barcelona, Spain (in planning)

Renovation of Aliados Avenue, Porto, Portugal, with Álvaro Siza (under construction)

## AWARDS

**1980**

António de Almeida Foundation

**1981**

Competition for the Casa des Artes, Porto – 1st prize

**1982**

Competition for the restructuring of the main square in Évora – 1st prize

**1984**

Antero de Quental Foundation

**1986**

Competition for the C.I.A.C. pavilions – 1st prize

**1987**

Competition for a Hotel in Salzburg – 1st prize

**1990**

IN/ARCH 1990, Sicily – 1st prize (ex-aequo)

**1992**

Secil Award for Architecture

Competition for the Construction of an Auditorium and a Children's Library in the City Hall Library of Porto – 1st prize

**1993**

The Stone in Architecture – 2nd prize

Secil Award for Architecture – Honorable Mention for the House in Alcanena, Torres Nova

National Awards for Architecture – Honorable Mention for the Cultural Centre and the House in Alcanena, Torres Nova

**1995**

The Stone in Architecture, Fiera di Verona – International Prize, for the House in Bom Jesus, Braga

**1996**

Annual award from the Portuguese Department of the International Association of Art Critics, for the building in Rua do Teatro, Porto

**1998**

IBERFAD Award – Nominee for the
  Pousada Santa Maria do Bouro,
  Amares
1st Biennale Ibero-American in
  Architecture and Civil Engineering, –
  1st prize for the Pousada Santa Maria
  do Bouro, Amares
Pessoa Award

**1999**

The Stone in Architecture Award –
  Honorable Mention for the Pousada
  Santa Maria do Bouro, Amares
Award FAD – Opinion Award for the Silo
  Cultural in Norteshopping, Matosinhos

**2001**

Heinrich-Tessenow Award – Gold Medal

**2002**

Nominee for the 3rd Biennale Ibero-
  American in Architecture and Civil
  Engineering, for the Courtyard Houses
  in Matosinhos, Porto

**2003**

The Stone in Architecture Award –
  Honorable Mention for the Project in
  waterfront of Matosinhos, Porto

**2004**

FAD Award – Finalist, for the Two
  Houses in Fomelos Ponte de Lima
Opinion Award of the FAD Jury
Secil Award for Architecture

European Award of Architecture from
the Economic European Comunity/
Mies van der Rohe Foundation,
Barcelona
Nominee for the following projects:
  1990 – Casa das Artes, Porto
  1992 – House in Alcanena,
  Torres Nova
  1994 – Department of Geosciences,
  Aveiro University
  1996 – Building in Rua do Teatro,
  Porto
  1998 – Pousada Santa Maria do
  Bouro, Amares
  2000 – Courtyard Houses in
  Matosinhos, Porto
  2002 – Cinema House for Manoel de
  Oliveira, Porto
Finalist for the following project:
  2005 – Braga Stadium, Braga

# EDUARDO SOUTO DE MOURA
## SELECTED BIBLIOGRAPHY

**1990**

*Eduardo Souto de Moura.* Wilfried Wang. Barcelona: Gustavo Gili Editorial SA

**1994**

*Eduardo Souto de Moura.* Luiz Trigueiros, ed. Texts by Antonio Angelillo and Paulo Pais. Lisbon: Editorial Blau

**1997**

*Eduardo Souto de Moura: Ten Houses.* Oscar Riera Ojeda. Gloucester, MA: Rockport Publishers Inc

**1999**

*Eduardo Souto de Moura – Temi di Progetti: Themes for Projects.* Laura Peretti, ed. Milan: Skira

**2000**

*Eduardo Souto de Moura.* Antonio Angelillo. Lisbon: Editorial Blau

**2001**

*Cool Construction: David Chipperfield, Eduardo Souto De Moura, Tod Williams and Billie Tsien, Waro Kishi.* Raymund Ryan. London: Thames & Hudson Ltd

*Eduardo Souto de Moura – Santa Maria do Bouro. Building a Pousada Using Stones from the Monastery.* Juan Hernandez Leon et al. Lisbon: White & Blue

**2003**

*Souto de Moura: Works and Projects.* Giovanni Leoni and Antonio Esposito. Milan: Electra Architecture

*Eduardo Souto de Moura.* Aurora Cuito and Cristina Montes, eds. London: teNeues Publishing UK Ltd

*Eduardo Souto de Moura: Stein Element Stone.* Werner Blaser. Basel: Birkhauser Verlag AG

*Eduardo Souto de Moura: Recent Work.* 2G no. 5 International Architecture Review. Monica Gili, ed. Text by Xavier Guell. Barcelona: Editorial Gustavo Gili SA

**2004**

*Great Spaces Small Houses.* Shigeru Ban, Álvaro Siza, Eduardo Souto de Moura. Corte Madera, CA: Gingko Press

*Eduardo Souto de Moura: Casa del Cine Manoel de Oliveira.* Jorge Figueira. Lisbon: Caleidoscópio

**2005**

*Eduardo Souto de Moura 1995–2005,* Texts by Luis Rojo de Castro, Madrid: El Croquis no 124

# CECIL BALMOND
## SELECTED BIOGRAPHY

**PROJECTS ARE LISTED UNDER THE YEAR OF THEIR FIRST CONCEPT PHASE; THE YEAR OF COMPLETION, IF DIFFERENT, IS NOTED IN PARENTHESIS.**

**1970**
Carlsberg Brewery, Northampton, UK. Architect: Knud Munk (1973)

**1975**
Masterplan for Qatar University, Doha, Qatar. Architect: RHWL Architects (1977)

**1978**
Staatsgalerie, Stuttgart, Germany. Architect: James Stirling (1984)

**1987**
Public Library, Latina, Italy. Architect: James Stirling/Michael Wilford & Associates ltd

**1988**
Museo Thyssen-Bornemisza, Madrid, Spain. Architect: Rafael Moneo Arquitecto (1992)
Kunsthal, Rotterdam, The Netherlands. Architect: OMA (1994)

**1989**
Congrexpo (Grand Palais), Lille, France. Architect: OMA (1994)

**1992**
Abando Passenger Interchange, Bilbao, Spain. Architect: James Stirling/Michael Wilford (1999)
Utrechtsebaan Office Building, The Hague, The Netherlands. Architect: Benthem Crouwel (1996)

**1993**
Bibliotheque de Jussieu, Paris, France. Architect: OMA

**1994**
Maison à Floirac Bordeaux, Aquitaine, France. Architect: OMA/Rem Koolhaas (1998)

**1995**
Portuguese Pavilion for Expo 98, Lisbon, Portugal. Architect: Álvaro Siza and Eduardo Souta de Moura (1998)
Project Study for Chemnitz Stadium, Germany. Architect: Peter Kulka/Ulrich Konigs (1996)
Masterplan for Universal City Complex, Los Angeles, USA. Architect: OMA
Togok - Feasibility Study, Seoul, Republic of South Korea. Architect: OMA
*Spiral* extension, Victoria & Albert Museum, London, UK. Architect: Daniel Libeskind

**1997**
Centraal Station, Arnhem, The Netherlands. Architect: UN Studio (2007)
Imperial War Museum, Salford, England. Architect: Daniel Libeskind.

**1998**
Illinois Institute of Technology, Student Centre, Chicago, Illinois, USA. Architect: OMA (2003)

Scottish Parliament Building, Holyrood, Edinburgh, UK. Architect: Enric Miralles (2004)

**1999**
MAB Tower, Rotterdam, The Netherlands. Architect: OMA (2001)
Jewish Museum San Francisco, USA. Architect: Daniel Libeskind/Gordon H Chong & Partners (2002)
University of Graz Music School, Austria. Architect: UN Studio
Seattle Central Library, USA. Architect: OMA/LMN Architects (2003)
Casa da Musica, Porto, Portugal. Architect: OMA (2005)

**2000**
Feasibility study for Kings Cross Station, London, UK. Architect: John McAslan & Partners ltd
Prada, Los Angeles, USA. Architect: OMA (2004)

**2001**
Los Angeles County Museum of Art, Los Angeles, USA. Architect: OMA
Uffizi Canopy, Florence, Italy. Architect: Arata Isozaki
Whitney Museum of American Art extension, New York, Architect: OMA
*Eighteen Turns*, Serpentine Gallery Pavilion, London, with Daniel Libeskind

# CECIL BALMOND
## SELECTED BIBLIOGRAPHY

**2002**

Serpentine Gallery Pavilion, London, UK, with Toyo Ito

*Marsyas*, Tate Modern, London, UK. Artist: Anish Kapoor (2003)

Chevasse Park, Liverpool, UK. Architect: Philip Johnson, Studio BAAD

**2003**

Selfridges, Glasgow, UK. Architect: Toyo Ito & Associates

Battersea Power Station Masterplan, London, UK, with Arup AGU (2006)

Grand Museum of Egypt, Giza, Cairo, Egypt. Architect: Heneghan Peng Architect (2009)

China Central Television (CCTV) Headquarters, Beijing, China, Architect: OMA/Rem Koolhaas, Ole Scheeren (2008)

**2004**

St Louis Forest Park, Missouri, USA. Architect: Shigeru Ban Architects (2006)

Centre Pompidou, Metz, France. Architect: Shigeru Ban Architects (2008)

Coimbra Footbridge, Mondego River, Coimbra, Portugal. Architect: António Adão da Fonseca, AFA (2005)

## BOOKS

**1998**

*Number 9: The Search for the Sigma Code*. Cecil Balmond . London: Prestel

*Unfolding - Nine Books in a Box*. Cecil Balmond and Daniel Libeskind. Rotterdam: NAi

**2002**

*Informal*. Cecil Balmond. London: Prestel

*Serpentine Gallery Pavilion 2002: Toyo Ito with Arup*. Cecil Balmond and Toyo Ito. Tokyo: Telescoweb

**2004**

*Concrete Poetry: Concrete Architecture in Australia*. Joe Rollo, foreword by Cecil Balmond. Sydney: Cement Concrete and Aggregates Australia

**2005**

*Informal* (Japanese edition). Cecil Balmond. Tokyo: TOTO

## ARTICLES

**1997**

'New Structure and the Informal', *Architectural Design*, Vol 67, No 9-10, September

**1998**

'How the Spiral will Stand Up', *The Times*, 2 December

**2000**

'The Generative Line', *Dialogue (Taiwan)*, December

**2001**

Jennifer Kabat, 'The Informalist', *Wired*, Issue 9.04, March

**2002**

Deyan Sudjic 'Take a Bow, Mr Balmond', *The Observer*, 27 October

Jay Merrick, 'The Engineer of Chaos', *Independent Review*, 28 December

**2004**

Hugh Pearman interview, 'Fresh Perspective', *Design Week*, 29 January

Jay Merrick, 'God of Big Things', *Independent on Sunday*, 8 August

Cecil Balmond and Toyo Ito in conversation, 'Concerning Fluid Spaces', *A+U*, Issue 2004.5, November

**2005**

Graham Bizley, 'The Rem and Cecil Show', *Building Design*, 29 April

# SUPPORTERS

THE SERPENTINE WOULD LIKE TO THANK THE INDIVIDUALS, TRUSTS, FOUNDATIONS AND COMPANIES WHOSE GENEROSITY ENABLES THE GALLERY TO REALIZE ITS ACCLAIMED EXHIBITION, ARCHITECTURE AND EDUCATION PROGRAMMES.

Netherlands Architecture Fund
The Dr Mortimer and Theresa
Sackler Foundation
The Rayne Foundation

**AND KIND ASSISTANCE FROM**
City of Westminster Arts Council
The Ernest Cook Trust
The Lone Pine Foundation
The Nyda and Oliver Prenn Foundation

**EXHIBITION PROGRAMME
SUPPORTED BY**
The Henry Moore Foundation

**EMERITUS BENEFACTOR**
Edwin C Cohen and
   The Blessing Way Foundation

**HONORARY PATRON**
Anthony Podesta, Podesta/Mattoon.com,
   Washington DC

**HONORARY BENEFACTORS**
Gavin Aldred
Mark and Lauren Booth
Ralph I Goldenberg
Noam and Geraldine Gottesman
Catherine and Pierre Lagrange
Stig Larsen
George and Angie Loudon
Lord Rothschild
Peter Simon
Debby and Peter Weinberg

**PATRONS**
Thomas Ammann Fine Art Zurich
Dr Bettina Bahlsen
Simon Bakewell and Cheri Phillips
Charles and Léonie Booth-Clibborn
Frances and John Bowes
Mr and Mrs Federico Ceretti
Dr Martin A Clarke
Sir Ronald and Lady Cohen
Terence and Niki Cole
Stevie Congdon and Harriet Hastings
Alistair Cookson and Vita Zaman
Carolyn Dailey
Thomas Dane Ltd
Robin and Noelle Doumar
Frank and Lorna Dunphy
Gagosian Gallery
Marian Goodman Gallery
David Gorton
Richard and Judith Greer
Sir Ronald Grierson
Richard and Odile Grogan
Jennifer and Matthew Harris
Katrin and Christoph Henkel
Galerie Max Hetzler, Berlin
Dorian Jabri
Tim Jefferies
Jennifer Kersis
Mr and Mrs Simon Lee
Vincent and Elizabeth Meyer
Alexandra Meyers
Mr Donald Moore
Dr Dambisa Moyo
Paul and Alison Myners
Guy and Marion Naggar

Ophiucus SA
Patrick Painter Gallery
Katherine Priestley and David Pitblado
Bob Rennie and Carey Fouks
Bruce and Shadi Ritchie
Kadee Robbins
David Roberts
Ruth and Richard Rogers
Alan and Joan Smith
John A Smith and Vicky Hughes
Lord Edward Spencer-Churchill
Speyer Family Foundation
Stan Stalnaker
Mr and Mrs David Stevenson
Ian and Mercedes Stoutzker
David Teiger
Laura and Barry Townsley
Jan Woroniecki
Poju and Anita Zabludowicz

**BENEFACTORS**
Heinz and Simone Ackermans
Shane Akeroyd
Max Alexander and
Anna Bateson
Alan and Charlotte Artus
Pedro C de Azambuja
James M Bartos
Anne Best
Roger and Beverley Bevan
Lavinia Calza Beveridge
David and Janice Blackburn
Anthony and Gisela Bloom
John and Jean Botts
Marcus Boyle

Vanessa Branson
Mrs Conchita Broomfield
Benjamin Brown
Mr and Mrs Charles Brown
Ossi and Paul Burger
John and Susan Burns
Marlene Burston
Mr and Mrs Philip Byrne
Jonathan and Vanessa Cameron
Jonathon P Carroll
Andrew Cecil
Monkey Chambers
Azia Chatila
Mr and Mrs Giuseppe Ciardi
Dr and Mrs David Cohen
Sadie Coles
Louise-Anne Comeau
Carole and Neville Conrad
Sulina and Matthew Conrad
Simon Copsey
Alexander Corcoran
Pilar Corrias and Adam Prideaux
Gul Coskun
Loraine da Costa
Mr and Mrs Cuniberti
Joan Curci
Linda and Ronald F Daitz
Helen and Colin David
Paul Davies
Ellynne Dec and Andrea Prat
Neil Duckworth
Adrienne Dumas
Denise Dumas
Lance Entwistle

Mike Fairbrass
Mr and Mrs Mark Fenwick
Harry and Ruth Fitzgibbons
Ruth Finch
David and Jane Fletcher
Bruce and Janet Flohr
Robert Forrest
Joscelyn and Edwin Fox
Eric and Louise Franck
Honor Fraser
James Freedman and Anna Kissin
Albert and Lyn Fuss
Lady Deedam Gaborit
Tatiana Gertik
Hugh Gibson
David Gill
Barbara Gladstone
Glovers Solicitors
Mr and Mrs John Gordon
Dimitri J Goulandris
Francesco Grana and Simona Fantinelli
Mrs Marcia Green
Richard and Linda Grosse
The Bryan Guinness Charitable Trust
Philip Gumuchdjian
Sascha Hackel and Marcus Bury
Abel G Halpern and Helen Chung-Halpern
Louise Hallett
Mr and Mrs Rupert Hambro
Mr and Mrs Antony Harbour
Susan Harris
Maria and Stratis Hatzistefanis
Mr and Mrs Rick Hayward
Thomas Healy and Fred Hochberg

Michael and Sarah Hewett
Mrs Samantha Heyworth
Marianne Holtermann
Mrs Juliette Hopkins
Mrs Martha Hummer-Bradley
Montague Hurst Charitable Trust
Mr Michael and Lady Miranda Hutchinson
Iraj and Eva Ispahani
Nicola Jacobs and Tony Schlesinger
Mrs Christine Johnston
Susie Jubb
John Kaldor and Naomi Milgrom
Howard and Linda Karshan
Malcolm King
James and Clare Kirkman
Tim and Dominique Kirkman
Mr and Mrs Charles Kirwan-Taylor
Mickey and Jeanne Klein
Herbert and Sybil Kretzmer
The Landau Foundation
Britt Lintner
Barbara Lloyd and Judy Collins
Peder Lund
Steve and Fran Magee
Mr Otto Julius Maier and Mrs Michèle
   Claudel-Maier
Claude Mandel and Maggie Mechlinski
Aniz Manji
The Lord and Lady Marks
Mr and Mrs Stephen Mather
James and Viviane Mayor
Warren and Victoria Miro
Susan and Claus Moehlmann
Jen Moores

Richard Nagy and Caroline Schmidt
Andrei Navrozov
Angela Nikolakopoulou
Marian and Hugh Nineham
Georgia Oetker
Tamiko Onozawa
Mr and Mrs Nicholas Oppenheim
Linda Pace
Desmond Page and Asun Gelardin
Maureen Paley
Dominic Palfreyman
Midge and Simon Palley
Kathrine Palmer
William Palmer
Dr M Max Parmar-Chauhan
Andrew and Jane Partridge
Julia Peyton-Jones
Ben and Georgie Pincus
George and Carolyn Pincus
Sophie Price
Mathew and Angela Prichard
Max Reed
Michael Rich
John and Jill Ritblat
Bruce and Shadi Ritchie
Jacqueline and Nicholas Roe
Victoria, Lady de Rothschild
James Roundell and Bona Montagu
Rolf and Maryam Sachs
Nigel and Annette Sacks
Michael and Julia Samuel
Isabelle Schiavi
Joana and Henrik Schliemann

Glenn Scott Wright
Martin and Elise Smith
Sotheby's
Mr and Mrs Jean-Marc Spitalier
Bina and Philippe von Stauffenberg
Simone and Robert Suss
Emma Tennant and Tim Owens
The Thames Wharf Charity
Christian and Sarah von Thun-Hohenstein
Britt Tidelius
Suzanne Togna
Emily Tsingou
Melissa Ulfane
Ashley and Lisa Unwin
David and Emma Verey
Mr and Mrs Ludovic de Walden
Darren J Walker
Audrey Wallrock
Rajan and Wanda Watumull
Pierre and Ziba de Weck
Daniel and Cecilia Weiner
Lord and Lady John Wellesley
Alannah Weston
Helen Ytuarte White
Charles and Kathryn Wickham
Robin Wight and Anastasia Alexander
Martha and David Winfield
Richard and Astrid Wolman
Mr and Mrs M Wolridge
Chad Wollen and Sian Davies
Nabil N Zaouk
Andrzej and Jill Zarzycki

SUMMIT GROUP
Vanessa Branson
Aud and Paolo Cuniberti
Colin and Helen David
Frank and Lorna Dunphy
Joscelyn, Jacqueline and Gerald Fox
Eric and Louise Franck
Honor Fraser
Richard and Odile Grogan
Jennifer and Matthew Harris
Iraj and Eva Ispahani
George and Angie Loudon
Mr Otto Julius Maier and Mrs Michèle
  Claudel-Maier
Bona Colonna Montagu
Jennifer Moores
Midge and Simon Palley
Oliver Prenn
Britt Tidelius
Helen Ytuarte White

And Patrons, Benefactors and Summit
Group members who wish to remain
anonymous

INTERNATIONAL MEDIA PARTNER
2004–05
Fortune

FUNDED BY
Arts Council of England
Westminster City Council

## SERPENTINE GALLERY PAVILION 2005
DESIGNED BY ÁLVARO SIZA AND EDUARDO SOUTO DE MOURA WITH CECIL BALMOND – ARUP
2 JULY – 2 OCTOBER 2005

This publication is sponsored by

The Pavilion is
supported by

| | Supply and Fabrication | Integrated Design | Advisors |
|---|---|---|---|
|  |  |  |  |

Platinum Sponsors

Gold Sponsors

Silver Sponsors

Bronze Sponsors

Serpentine Gallery
Kensington Gardens
London
W2 3XA

Telephone +44 (0)20 7402 6075
Fax +44 (0)20 7402 4103
www.serpentinegallery.org

This book was produced and published by
the Serpentine Gallery, London and Trolley, London
www.trolleybookscom

Project Director Julia Peyton-Jones
Project Co-ordinators: Rebecca Morrill, Anna Lopriore
Edited by Melissa Larner
Designed by Fruitmachine

Repro by Fotolito Express
Printed in Italy by Soso Industrie Grafiche Spa

ISBN 1-905190-03-4 (Serpentine Gallery, London)
ISBN 1-904563-48-1 (Trolley)

Photographs © 2005

Ludwig Abache
Arup/OMA
Arup/Christian Richters
Cecil Balmond
Gabriele Basilico
Richard Bryant/arcaid.co.uk
Deborah Bullen
Alessandra Chemollo
Luis Ferreira Alves
Tiago Figueiredo
Dennis Gilbert/VIEW
Hugo Glendinning
Mark Robinson
Stephen White

Drawings © 2005

Álvaro Siza
Eduardo Souto de Moura
Cecil Balmond

The Serpentine Gallery is funded by